# *Living with*
# TIME TO
# THINK

## *The goddaughter letters*

*Because They Can Think For Themselves*

*Living with*

# TIME TO THINK

*The goddaughter letters*

*Because They Can Think For Themselves*

## NANCY KLINE

An Hachette UK Company
www.hachette.co.uk

First published in Great Britain in 2014 by
Cassell, a division of Octopus Publishing Group Ltd
Endeavour House
189 Shaftesbury Avenue
London
WC2H 8JY
www.octopusbooks.co.uk

ISBN 978-1-84403-795-7

A CIP catalogue record for this book is available from the British Library

Printed and bound by CPI Group (UK) Ltd, Croydon, CR0 4YY
10 9 8 7 6 5 4 3 2 1

Publisher: Denise Bates
Art Director: Yasia Williams-Leedham
Design: Jeremy Tilston
Production Controller: Sarah Kramer

For Hattie, Kimberley and Meghan
With my love

# Contents

# Kimberley

# Introduction

When they were young, each of my goddaughters asked me a question. The questions dazzled me. I needed to think about them. And I promised that someday I would answer. I hoped I would find a way that would be worthy of the questions. It took me many years.

I decided I could answer best through a collection of letters to each of them, which at different stages in their lives I completed and offered as a gift.

The three questions sprang from three very different girls at different ages. But each cradled a common, uncompromising theme: the injunction to think for yourself. Each question leapt with wild amounts of courage into the world of independent thinking.

And so the letters became an invitation to each girl to venture into her own mind, to listen to her own heart, to shape her own life.

As personal as the questions were, as focused as I was on the particular goddaughter as I wrote, the timeless nature of our conversation seemed to speak to any age. And we agreed that I would offer these letters now as a gift to you and to the people, young women or otherwise, who matter most to you.

These letters also witness my belief that it is the job of one generation to encourage the next. Specifically it is our job to encourage them to think for themselves. Most of their lives they are told not to. And their questions languish, unformed and unanswered.

'Living with time to think' is a demanding proposal. It may sound like time management. But it is not. It is a recognition that life itself should be a time of thinking, a time most crucially of thinking for ourselves. My 35 years of researching and teaching the conditions for people of all ages to do just that have convinced me that independent thinking, while still often forbidden, is the one thing on which everything else depends.

## Life itself should be a time most crucially of thinking for ourselves.

The concept of the 'Thinking Environment' and my two 'Time to Think' books express this in the context of work and society. Living with Time to Think takes the concept to another, more personal level.

Young people do want to do their own thinking. They don't want us to grab them and drag them somewhere of our choosing. They want only our insights that will immediately lead them to their own.

They want to walk upright, at their own pace, down roads we could never have envisioned for them, taking risks we do not understand. They want to arrive somewhere new, having shaped on their way a world of their own generation, a world more compassionate and intelligent than ours.

I hope these letters point in that direction. But my answers are only to consider, not to swallow whole. Godmothers are no fonts. We are just certain people who love certain other people with all our hearts, and are honoured to be asked such big questions.

# Meghan

## When I get to be a woman, how can I have a good life?

When Meghan was ten, she was a passionate reader. As a young Quaker she had also heard in her school and family about equality and about the courage to live for peace. One day as she was reading, her little brother darted through the living room, making ack-ack sounds and pointing a make-believe gun at the ceiling. Meghan looked up. She frowned and sighed, 'Why do boys do stupid stuff like that?'

'Long story,' I said.

She went back to her book. A few minutes passed. Then she closed the book and was quiet. She looked over at me and said, 'Nancy, when I get to be a woman, how can I have a good life?'

Moved by the far reach of her question, I was quiet, too. Finally I told her I would get back to her about that one day. Maybe, I said, I would write her a letter.

# Hattie

## Given that we all die, how do we find meaning in living?

Just before Christmas each year I took Hattie shopping to choose her present. I was building for her, as my mother had for me, a collection of bone china 'odd' cups and saucers. Each year Hattie chose a different style and designer. My job was to drive her there and heroically say nothing while she chose.

Hattie was 12. On this trip through the Oxfordshire countryside, she said out of the comfortable quiet between us, 'Nancy, given that we all die, how do we find meaning in living?'

I was thrown, as I had been with Meghan, by the enormity of her question. I knew that she had lived through the possibility that her triplet brother would die from a brain tumour. And she had comforted me when my twin brother died from the same thing. Death had fallen into her life.

But this question was bigger even than that. I groped, and ultimately I told her I would think seriously about it and would one day offer her whatever insights I could. Maybe, I said, I would write her a letter.

# Kimberley

## Today – how can we be happy?

Pondering Meghan's and Hattie's questions some time later, I remembered that many years before, Kimberley, my niece and first goddaughter, had been first also to ask me a startling question. She was five at the time. She and I were on a drive under the New Mexico skies.

Out of nowhere she said, 'Aunt Nancy, today – how can we be happy?'

It was a question of the moment, but also of the ages. Although only five, she seemed, in pre-developed ways, already to see that the world prescribes a certain kind of happiness, happiness defined by others. 'How can we be happy today?' was no ordinary 'What can we do today?' question. It revealed, it seemed to me, an unconscious awareness of the practised elusiveness of this most prized of states.

I told her, much later in her life, that I was writing her a letter about that.

# Meghan

When I get to be a woman,
how can I have a good life?

# Dear Meghan
## Introduction

When you were ten years old, I told you I would write something for you, something you could hold close to your heart, that you could turn to for backbone when feeling beguiled, count on to hold your hand when the light dims and the way recedes, and beckon you to joy no matter what.

I said this to you because you had said to me, 'Nancy, when I am a woman, how can I have a good life?' I was silenced by the question, by its importance and by your very grown-up concern. So, stalling, I said to you, 'Meghan, I promise I will think about that.'

'When?' you asked.

'Well, I'll tell you what. I will write you a letter about that someday,' I said.

'Oh, good,' you said, 'when?'

After more silence, having no idea whether I ever could answer that question as fully or dependably as you deserved, I said, hugging you, 'I don't know for sure; but I promise I will.'

That was eight years ago. Now you are graduating from high school. And over that time I have written what I hope will be a friend for you. I offer it to you now, on the threshold of womanhood, as your sights soar towards a grown-up life, gracing the earth with your fine mind, your highly hewn awareness of others, your self-discipline, your outrage at injustice and your insistence on time to think and feel and decide things for yourself. With this book comes my love.

You asked me for advice. That is a siren's moment. We think we know exactly what others need. And to be asked for advice is alluring. But with difficulty I resisted. I don't really approve of it. I earn most of my living advising (paradoxically) against it. I encourage people (and you now) to think for themselves.

To do that we simply have to refuse to give advice. Only if the person has done their own thinking in our riveted, generative silence first (and has gobs of ideas of their own to show for it), and only if they beg us, can we even consider suggesting what they might do.

This is because most of the time advice is infantilizing. It treats people like children (including children). And that keeps them from thinking for themselves. Advice asks one person to become the other.

> ## Advice asks one person to become the other.

In that way it too often poisons the soil of the never-before-thought-of thought and is, therefore, probably one reason our world staggers. We are assuming that if we keep on coming up with the same ideas and doing the same things in the same way, somehow the results will be different. Fortunately, the world now sees this as one sign of madness.

In other words, advice by its nature assumes that what went before is good enough for what is needed now. But as there are hardly even two molecules alike in the entire universe, it is highly unlikely that what one person found helpful or elucidating in one complex moment of their life will be more than slightly useful in a differently complex moment of another's.

So advice is out.

But experience is in. And so is knowledge. They work. They open possibilities and nurture independent thinking. They say, 'Consider me; then take me or leave me.'

So I offer to you here my experience and my limited knowledge. You can do with it what you want, including highlighting it and dragging it decisively into the trash.

Because, actually, even taking care to use only the language of experience and knowledge I should nevertheless resist altogether and just say to you right now, 'I'll stop writing and come to your house, sit on your bed with you and listen beautifully while you come up with ideas for a good life that I have never thought of.' Then we could put all of those ideas into a book, wrap it with a golden ribbon and one day you could open it and marvel at the wisdom.

But when you were still under five feet tall, on your fourth reading of the entire 'Babysitter' series, before bras or boys or lacrosse or SATs, I told you I would write you something. And a deal is a deal. So I want you to have it now as you graduate from high school, and for the rest of your life, long after I am dead, even if it only occasionally grazes your life with relevance or applicability. I hope I have done your question justice. You have honoured me by asking it.

Life is short. It is melodious and wondrous. At times it is callous. At its best it requires the best from us. And so, should you someday want to ask me again how, as a woman, you can have a good life, here is what I would say to you.

# Dear Meghan
## One

### Thinking For Yourself

I met with a group of six girls last month. They were there, on a Young Women As Leaders workshop, to think about expanding their student government.

We began with a simple question: 'What do you think needs to be done?' No one spoke. I asked them again. Nothing. And these were high-achieving, Harvard-in-their-sights 17-year-olds. Then one of them said, 'Beats me. What do you guys think?' (Why do girls call each other guys?) She pointed to her friends. They just looked at each other.

This is not the first time this has happened in the presence of that question. These leadership workshops usually begin here, with that blank look staring back at that simple question. The workshops encourage young people to think for themselves and to help each other do that. This scene was familiar.

In fact, leaders of all ages, when asked in the presence of their peers to say what they really think, often go blank in the eyes like that. I see this in corporate meetings and in boardrooms long after teenage conformity, long after Harvard and way too close to the end of life.

'What do you think, really?' I ask. They squirm. I ask again. Eventually they speak. But the time-lapse says everything.

Our world rarely wants to know what we really think; no one asks, and so we do not know; and so we plough on, task-focused midwives to the repetitive ideas of others. As a result, what we really think needs careful resurrecting because virtually every adult life has buried it. Schools and faith groups and professionals, not just parents, help in the burial, too – too often, too sadly, too inadvertently and sometimes too on purpose.

> You, and only you, can do your own thinking.

You, and only you, can do your own thinking. No one else can discover your thoughts, your perceptions, your insights. And no one else can make your decisions as well as you can after the discovery.

So more than anything I hope you will treasure the incomprehensibly superb capacity to think that makes you so specially human, and so specially Meghan.

A good life depends on it.

# Dear Meghan
## Two

### Your Purpose

Your primary reference point deserves to be a growing knowledge of why you are here. This knowledge is intact. It is inside you. It arrived when you did, complete with its own intelligence, as you entered the world. It waits for you and is instantly responsive when you consult it. It needs only to be awakened through your careful attention to its signals. It speaks the truth about what you can accomplish best, about what will lead you to joy, what will give your moments meaning and your life impact, about what you must require anyone who deserves your love to celebrate wholeheartedly – and never, ever to denigrate.

Is this thing I am about to do elegantly in line with the essence of me?

The knowledge of why you are here plays no games, wrings no ransom, longs for nothing except its own fulfilment. It is the greatest generator of ease in all of life's designs. You can refer to it, regardless of your starting point, regardless of your fear, regardless of the prognosis, regardless of the brows of caution, regardless of the question.

You have already begun to do this. You have chosen a university that can help you develop your talents, the things that engage you most. You already are noticing what kind of work gives you joy and will use you well. You know what you love to learn. You know what you need to do to feel your energy growing. This is a wonderful thing.

This question goes beautifully with every decision you make for the rest of your life, and is essential for the good life you as a woman can establish:

In doing this, will I be able to contribute, to achieve, to discover, to offer to people and to the world, an expression of my purpose in being alive?

Is this thing I am about to do elegantly in line with the essence of me?

The answer will honour you. It and your integrity are the only two things that deserve your gracious obedience.

# Dear Meghan
## Three

## Nothing So Intimate

Let's do men a favour. Let's not expect them to be better than we are. They're not. Not inherently. Not just because they are men. Let's stop expecting them to be, so that we can spare them our disappointment when we find out they are not.

One of the worst things we do to men is to walk backward into adulthood expecting men to save us from the demands of our own excellence and competence, longing (however unconsciously) for them to shoot us up with the feeling of being small and protected, finding our meaning and worth in their eyes.

The world (even in this post-feminist, post-modern, post-everything era) has been telling you in your sleep and in your every waking moment, in most ads and videos (yes, even in *Gilda the Magnificent*) that however high women may rise in CNN or Congress, however precisely men might share the ironing, the dish-washing, the dribble-dabbing, the scalpel, the gavel, the pulpit or the cockpit, women are to expect men, just because they are men, to do that deep-down, fairy-tale, kissing-awake, rescuing, white-charger, glass-slipper thing – to lift us away from our self-sufficiency with their 'particularly male' last-minute saving of the day, offering us the ultimate confirmation: that because they want us, we as women are acceptable and valued, good enough, desirable and okay.

The myth is that men, after all, are superior to women in some non-crystalline, intrinsic sense. God said so. (And he should know because he is a man.)

The world does this a bit more surreptitiously than it did 20 years ago. Its key agent these days is the message inside organizations and politics that, sure, women are welcome here, but to enter they will have to leave their culture behind and take on men's culture. Come on in if you aspire to, they say to us; but get ready to become like us.

What?, they say to us later when we offer an alternative to the damage some of their culture causes them and us and world policy, you want us to be like you? Men's culture to incorporate women's culture? Um, probably not a good idea. We have goals, you know, and we have to reach our targets and please our shareholders and constituencies and win, win, win; and frankly, we don't have lots of time for, well, fluff. And anyway, if we as men seriously considered women's culture as a superb component to real success in the world, we would be seen as gay, and that is just 100 per cent not okay thank you very, very much, good night.

Women and men are, in any sense that matters at all, inherently equal.

The message that men (just because they are men) should dictate the rules is in the DNA of most advertising, too. How many designer ice cream advertisements have you seen, for example, in which the ice cream equates gorgeous sex with a beautiful woman who is as strong, smart, forward-looking and in charge as the beautiful man who is also as tender and surrendering as the beautiful woman? Zero. Instead, typically the woman is carried off by the man with her head flung back, eyes rolling inside her eyelids, smeared with a not-so-subtle creamy drip on her chin. Sex is to follow this conquest, and she is to partake, gratefully stupefied.

However bombarded your life continues to be by the carnivorous world of gender conditioning, please consider that being knocked off balance by a man does not ensure a thing: not a life of satisfaction or meaning nor a single second of wonderful sex; and it certainly does not set you both up to engage with each other irrepressibly, or to know the deepest chambers of real love, or to talk and laugh into the night.

In fact, take into your heart this observation: gender conditioning is a Möbius strip of untrue assumptions (a.k.a. lies). It has nothing to do with inherent quality or healthy culture. And take in the irony: men strive to be the very set of things that kill them in the end. This is particularly sad because none of those things (being tough and feeling nothing and leading ruthlessly and taking up all the space and killing) is inherently male anyway. These are behaviours imbedded in men by messages and conditioning, and sometimes by force, from the moment anyone knows they are male.

Women and men are, in any sense that matters at all, inherently equal: equally good, equally intelligent, equally loving, resourceful, smart, ambitious, able to lead, solve problems, think big, fix cars, raise children, write, care, bless the dead, run the A & E, mow the lawn, feel a feeling and get the skin off garlic in one motion. We are both genetically deeply connected to our hearts, to our fondest dreams of peace for the world, to our talent to write software, read genes and chip away magically at marble.

If you just accept that men are not going to save you or give you meaning, because you do not need to be saved and because you came equipped with your own meaning, if you resist even a tiny pull to be resurrected by, outshone by or drop-dead impressed by a man just because he is a man, you will do men possibly the biggest favour in the world: you will not be disappointed in them. That would be a relief for every man on the planet. Otherwise, you will, in that inside place where things are jumbled and not articulated, expect a man to hold you in his superior arms at every crucial moment. And when you wake, not to his kiss but to his humanity, and realize that he cannot and never will be able to replace your inherent effectiveness with his, you may be tempted to resent him for it.

If you long for that Hollywood high of collapsing into men's power, and then they drop you, you will be furious. But that will have been your doing – because they were never strong enough to hold you in the first place. Only you are strong enough to hold you.

Disappointment is painful. But it is also powerless. It is the view from the victim's porch.

This truth is liberating: there is no Prince Charming; there is no white horse; there is no glass slipper; and no kiss, however delicious and tender and trustworthy, can ever bring you back to life. Only you can bring you back to life.

So let's let men be men, people, you know, just ordinary beings, wonderful much of the time, complete with gunshot wounds in their hearts from their often relentless conditioning. Let's admire them for the ways many of them have stood up to that conditioning and refused to absorb it. Let's admire them for the moments when they have pulled out those lies' leechy feet that raped the skin of their souls when they were not looking. We can admire them, as we do women, for the human beings they are. But let's not expect them to be better than we are.

Then should you find yourself in the chamber of the United Nations or in the Chair of Number One Global Inc., you won't be surprised to find that the men there are not better than you, either. You won't need to criticize them for that. It is possible for a man to look up to you without your having to look down on him.

Most important, perhaps, it is possible to know that men do not have to be better than you in order for them to be good in your eyes.

I remember the morning I woke up and realized this. I was 35. I was furious at an important man in my life. And within a few minutes of feeling that rage, I became devastated by the unexpected, crushing insight that he was not superior to me. I realized in that place that harbours all storybook hope and grown-up denial, that I had, since I had met him, expected him to be better, wiser, stronger than I was. Inherently. Because he was a man. There was a chill about that moment.

I remember thinking that one of two things was true. Either I was a kind of subspecies because the only way you can keep someone in a superior position to you when they are falling is to fall faster and further than they do. Or I was, after all, inherently as good as he was; and that idea I knew would turn my world upside down.

I felt completely alone.

I experienced for several months a kind of withdrawal from a lifetime of fixes. This expectation that men are inherently better than we are is a drug because it is offers a surge of artificial wellbeing, and then it empties you.

But facing it was worth it because I discovered for myself that when you are just you, what men do, or think of you, cannot destroy you. It cannot create you, either, and so you have virtually infinite possibilities of what to do and be in your life.

You can happily live with men, marry them, work with them, make love, dance, cook, create children, set policy, make decisions, stock shelves and accumulate a fortune with them. But you do not need them in order to be good enough.

And you do not need to emulate the rigid, destructive behaviours in their culture. You don't need to confuse leadership with competition and control. Or let admiration for men as men lure you down that 'we must do it the way they do if we want to be successful' road. The world is haemorrhaging because of that model of leadership. You can figure out a better model. And you can invite men to join you, to emulate your culture and weave in the flexible, intelligent parts of theirs, to create a new world.

So, for men's sake, and for yours, you can be a woman not surprised at her own excellence. A woman who does not hold herself back for fear her success will make a man look bad, for fear she will then have to face the end of the fairy tale. A woman who exults in the inherent equality of both genders and promotes the best of both gender cultures. A woman who enjoys deep and abiding and even delicious relationships with men. A phenomenal woman who defies disappointment and successfully resists resentment.

You are neither diminished nor authenticated by a man.

Thank goodness.

There is nothing so intimate as equality.

# Dear Meghan

## Four

### Intelligent Worship

I wonder what you worship. Or if you do. I know what you don't worship. You do not worship wealth or winning or words without roots. And I know that as a Quaker you are no advocate for anthropomorphic absurdity. But you do speak of things of the spirit. And I wonder whether you worship that and what it is to you. I do not seek to disturb it. I respect it. I wonder about it, and I honour it. And I know that, anyway, this asserted dimension is by definition untouchable. So I will leave it orbiting out of our reach.

> To worship your integrity is to escape the enslavement of worship. Your integrity is your only safe altar.

As I do, I propose that intelligent worship (oxymoron or paradox?) starts and lives inside the worshipper. To the extent that you worship anything, you do so from inside you. You know whatever it is first, and only, through your body. That is all you have. What your body tells you about this supra-logical, ineffable dimension of life is all you know of it.

So if you did not make it up yourself, your self most surely presented it to you. At the very least your self is the conduit, the code-breaker. And so your experience of it is pure, is true, only if your experience of you is pure and true. If this worshipped spirit is important to you, the integrity of you must be important to you, too, so important that you access your integrity first and hold it in reverence first. It is your channel to truth.

Your integrity, your inner voice, your incorruptible self are the starting place, it seems to me, for intelligent worship. This is because worship, a state of unquestioned veneration, is a dangerous path. By definition it requires obedience, and obedience edges toward annihilation of self. And so paradoxically, in order to worship intelligently, we must start where worship is defied by the worshipped object itself.

Your integrity is such an object. Integrity by definition is whole, complete, integrated. And so to worship your integrity is to escape the enslavement of worship; it is to shun unquestioned obedience; it is to think for yourself. It allows you then to know what else is worthy of your reverence.

Your integrity instructs you, it does not command you. It thrives on the courage of your own questions, on the clarity of your own mind. It depends for its life on the depth of your own heart, on your decision to face rather than turn away, and on your ability to find quiet inside you.

Your integrity exists. Physics and archaeology will never disprove it.

Your integrity is current and always relevant. It needs no ancient creed to give it credibility.

Your integrity is immediately available to you. It does not sway precariously on the mast of multiple, conflicting interpretations or translations.

Your integrity needs no infrastructure. Power struggles, titles, rituals and riches do not express it or house it or threaten it. And so it can never become the beatified justification for slaughter. It can only give life. It guides you if you ask. And if you listen, like lumens it leads you from this certain moment into your always-forming future. It hands you to your longed-for good life.

Your integrity also protects you from unworthy worship. It scoops you up from the feet of gurus and the pedlars of ultimism, from totems, from Eliot's human voices, from the postponement of discipline and from the abandoning of your body to chance.

Your integrity is first and forever. It warrants worship. And if it turns out that something extra-human does surpass the wonders of the diastole and systole, it probably does so through the red real heart of you.

Your integrity is your only safe altar.

# Dear Meghan
## Five

### Return To Solitude

Can you live alone? Not forever. But for a while?

Don't misunderstand. I think that living with a person you love is a joy not to be missed, one worth all the adjustments and givings to make the joys dominate. But for a time at least, and if we have a chance, living alone can, ironically, make us gems to live with.

This good-for-living-with outcome of living alone emerges because in a particular kind of solitude you can explore the startling fact that you exist – fully and in your own right.

Knowing you exist, which you may think is dismissibly obvious, is one of the most embarrassingly unobvious, truly great challenges and fine accomplishments of womanhood, one met rarely. You know you exist at this way-down, certain, nothing-can-shake-you level when you do not need any other person to confirm this; when

You can hear in solitude what is silenced by socializing.

you do not need to hitch up with, live with or hear positive things from another person to confirm your absolute, beautiful self, your inherent right to be alive, the special, never-before-designed, valuable existence that is you.

And no man, no woman, no election, no job, no medal, no newspaper profile, no therapist and, most important, no living-with-partner can confirm this. It is just plain true every second. You uniquely exist. Living alone can help you confirm this.

This happens partly because living alone gives you a chance to figure out how you like things, what making a home means to you, how you prefer to design the evening, organize the spices, invest the money, feed the hibiscus – if for once it is just you making the decisions. This is part of knowing you exist. You decide. You do it.

And if there is emptiness there, or fear, a kind of wariness of the presence of just you, you can pay attention to that. You can talk to it. You can let it morph from addiction-to-others into acceptance-of-you.

If you have a period of time, a year maybe, when you have to be your own companion, you will have a chance of liking that companion. If you have it early, you will have it for a reference point all your life. And then in some part of you, you will always welcome time with yourself.

I know women who have gone through their whole lives never enjoying their right to be alive and alone, 'doing nothing'. They feel they have the right to exist only if they are needed and busy. When someone needs them, especially in a crisis, a part of them feels relieved because they know what to do and they do not have to make choices for themselves. I know women, in fact, who live from crisis to crisis (real or imagined) and who feel frightened when everything is fine.

Being with yourself can then also be possible when you are with others. I don't mean that you should be self-absorbed. I mean that when you are with people, fully engaged, you can refer to yourself, not to them, for evidence of your existence. You can then see that you and they are not the same people and that your existence does not depend upon their embrace of you. Knowing that, you can truly see them and hear them and know that you have lived that moment with them fully. And you will be much better company.

Can you know that you exist without one other person or need telling you that you do?

What happens for you when nothing demands your attention? Does guilt lurk? Is 'being' your friend?

Can you wake at dawn to that mad rush of bird joy, lie there and just listen?

Or, in order to feel alive, do you have to have your iPhone on, or a project in your bag, or a list to make, in case the bus is late and you have an unplanned moment on your hands?

Can you go home after your day's work and just sit for a moment, not click on the TV or check Facebook or even talk to anyone?

You read for pleasure when you are alone, Meghan. That is

> Can you wake at dawn to that mad rush of bird joy, lie there and just listen?

important. Some people cannot allow themselves to read at all, and some only for work or improvement. Some people consider reading a gift they don't deserve because they have not helped enough people yet, or made enough money yet, or finished their 'work' yet, or tucked everyone in.

So I am glad you read, and that you love it. (One of my favourite memories is of you and your favourite book curled up in the booth at Lee's Kitchen, happy to escape the endless conversation between your mother and me.)

But even reading is busy, and so it would be good to know that you can put the book down and just be, now and then.

How much of your world can you caress by wrapping it around you with nothing at all to acknowledge you in this moment?

Living alone can give you experience of this. It can give you time to be, without being with. It can require you to notice the moment in ways that elude you when you are meeting others' needs, however subtly.

Should you have children one day, they, too, will be grateful for your solitude and for the clarity that emerges from it that it is you, not they, that holds the key to your good life. Lives lived through children lead children away from their lives. Children want their parents not to need them to fulfil the dreams the parents should have pursued for themselves. Healthy mothering requires time alone.

## No one else will ever be you. Isn't that wonderful?

You will die someday. You exist now. If there is no world beyond this very physical one, how much of it will you wish you had noticed if you die? How much of you will you have wanted to know?

And if there is a vast existence of which this life is only one small moment, what will you be able to say about it when you move on? Will it be only: in this life I fulfilled needs? Or might it include: I knew life deeply; I noticed it because I was alone, and still?

And then, when you are living with your beloved, you can remember to return to solitude. You can seek it not for escape, but to remember that you exist and are enough. You can let it show you that all fibres of life are touched by you and you by them, regardless of what you are doing.

You can hear in solitude what is silenced by socializing.

You can see in solitude what is visible when interaction does not sully the view.

No one else will ever be you. Isn't that wonderful? It is only you that is this particular exquisite and worthy and irresistible Meghan, lovely, brainy, able to sing, to wonder, to know, explore, lead and then sit in undisturbed solitude, all on the same day.

In solitude you can learn not to lose yourself in others. And in solitude you can rout your fear of losing them. Solitude reminds you that *you* are the person who neither ingests you nor leaves you. Solitude reminds you that you have you forever. And knowing that, you can return to deep connection to others, holding yourself close as your most respectful and permanent partner, present and kind, making healthy the loving of others because there is no you to lose in the loving.

# Dear Meghan
## Six

## The Right To Be Right

There are some ancient injunctions that resound with freshness and are so demanding of our best that few of us ever really achieve them. And so they last and last, never worn. They are the good in a good life. 'Love thy neighbour as thyself' is one of them.

But 'love thy neighbour as thyself' does not mean 'love thy neighbour as if they were thyself'. It means love them for who they really are, as well as you love yourself and as well as you would want them to love you.

Love of this dimension also means more than not hating. It means more than tolerance, more than allowing people to join us, more than not silencing them. It requires us to listen, to want to know. 'It requires us,' a friend quoted once, 'to grant to others not just the right to be heard but, more profoundly, the right to be right.'

This idea jars. We stay clear of it. It is unapproachable because we think deep down that we are right. We preach diversity, respect and love in our schools and government and management theories. But we impose ourselves.

We are afraid to listen. We are afraid we might hear something disturbingly sensible, maybe even inspired, that does not fit us. We are afraid that we will not know what to do with what we hear. We cannot consider considering it, deeply, seriously, dangerously. How can we respect people different from us, we then reason unconsciously, given that we are right?

Conversion is our habitual response to difference. And to that end we tell others what they should want, what they should believe, who they are, why they do what they do; and we define for them the possibilities life holds. We hold open to them doors of our choosing, doors to our life. Doors to our culture. We wave to them, then usher them, then force them in.

A radical level of respect for all human beings, so close to the heart of the US Bill of Rights and to the laws of Moses, to the teachings of Jesus of Nazareth, to the doctrine of Mohammed and the philosophy of the Buddha, we are not about to embrace. To contemplate the possibility, to let in even a second's thought, that they-who-are-different-from-us might be more than just welcome, they might be right, would bring into question, and require us to think about, every single premise on which we have imposed our missiles, our money, our food chains, our drugs, our merchandise and our lies for millennia. Surely we are right. Surely our god did declare it our duty to colonize and clone. Surely we are the chosen ones, the right ones, the bearers of answers to life's big questions. Surely.

> We preach diversity, but we impose ourselves.

Surely not, I would hope. Surely not, dearest Meghan, heiress to this world created for you by us, your parental generation, and by our parents and their parents and theirs and theirs and theirs. All of us inherit the war against difference and uniqueness and peace, another kind of war against thinking for ourselves. Another kind of war against a deeply good life.

I propose that we change that legacy. Starting today. I propose that from this moment to the next and the next and all the nexts down all of the ages to come, we begin to offer to your generation the legacy of independent thinking, the realm of being human and of humans being together so that we are our real selves, thinking our real thoughts, hearing each other's real hearts and hopes – without fear, able to think of new designs for living together.

On the evening of 9/11, rising from my chair after four hours of adhesive TV coverage of planes melting buildings and cratering the earth, of ash, hurled bodies and the recorded voices of the dead, I walked to the window and noticed a thought as it scampered, camouflaged as fantasy, across my mind. 'What if,' I wondered, 'this time the leaders of the world, particularly the US and Islamic worlds, could agree to gather immediately in a room somewhere neutral, close the door and listen to each other answer these questions without interruption and with a deep and genuine longing to know what each other truly thought, for as long as it took:

> Conversion is our habitual response to difference.

Why did this happen?

What was each of us assuming that led to this atrocity?

What would we have to assume instead in order for this never to happen again?

If we were to build, from this point on, a world in which all human beings were granted respect and the right to be right, what would we do first to build peace?

What would have to change in order for us to trust each other that intelligently?

But scampering is no way for an idea to fire up a heart. A heavy heart needs confidence, clarity, courage to be convinced. So the idea skulked away, and I returned to the devastating, gruesome and flag-waving, self-righteous, wronged and violated view saturating the TV coverage that I knew would soon dictate military revenge. Revenge because, as we know, we are right.

But recently, I was asked to give a talk called 'The Thinking Environment as a Framework For Peace'. And that night in Oxford, in front of a log fire and 50 people, I posed those five questions.

And today with new energy I ask myself again: what would need to happen so that next time there is a provocation that clamours for revenge, leaders can choose to gather and think and bestow attention upon each other? The sort of attention that is born of deep interest and respect as human beings, thinking so rigorously and creatively that their brains ache, rather than collapsing into the savage state of 'being right' and deciding to kill again?

> Peace springs from an unquenchable need to find out what others really think.

This is not a question I impose upon you, Meghan. As my mother said to me, 'I apologise for the mess my generation has imposed upon yours. I just hope we have given you a measure of courage to face what we have done, and a measure of hope to do something about it. But remember, it was not your fault. It all began long before you were born.'

You are a young woman of peace. I know this because it springs from every look, every word, every beat of your heart. Wherever you walk, whatever you do, you lay seeds of peace, just because you are there being you. You do not have to do anything special to make peace around you; you just have to be Meghan. Your particular self is that good.

But because it is your graduation and because it never hurts to propose a widening circle of influence in someone's dreams, I offer you additionally a gift of hope and courage to have an impact beyond your visible horizons.

I offer you also, whenever you want it, my attention to think about what you might do to expose the world to peace as you understand it. And I offer you a conscious Thinking Environment, a framework that might have at least some value in bringing all human beings back to each other with respect and with the hunger to know each other's real selves.

I believe that peace springs not from fear or ultimatums, and certainly not from 'being right' and killing, but rather from an unquenchable need to find out what others, safe enough to say, really think and want and need, and from those perspectives to sharpen, alter, broaden and embolden our solutions together.

All of this comes with my deepest respect for the young woman that you are and the young dreams you harbour.

# Dear Meghan

## Seven

### Waiting Until Thursday

My mother's voice lives inside me. 'Choose your battles,' she said at just the right junctures. I watched her do that with her life. She was good at it. And when she chose, she fought with a flourish and won.

Those three words, Meghan, could turn out to be your best friend. They mean: decide what matters to you; recognize that you cannot manufacture enough time or energy to fight every single issue you may want to fight in life and that credibility will drain from your stances if your stances are too many and undifferentiated.

So you can decide what matters most and fight for those things. The other battles you can leave to others. You also can then live happily enough and with considerable self-respect in the face of those battles you do not choose to fight. Choosing does not mean surrender. It signals discernment.

Waiting until Thursday is a cousin of this view. Or rather, it is a road to it. It is a good way to figure out which battles to choose. And it recognizes that emotional honesty comes in many forms, and that emotional health in a relationship is not always nurtured by instant reactions. It also recognizes that living in a state of irritation and criticism and anger is no way to live.

I started 'waiting until Thursday' one Saturday when I noticed that Christopher had moved my mother's priceless Steuben crystal vase from the conservatory table into a cupboard. I was devastated.

I took the vase in my arms, pressed it to my breast, leaned over it and cried. I talked to my mother, dead nearly 15 years, telling her how much I loved her and missed her, and how beautiful I thought the vase was, how elegant it always looked on the living-room table in our home in New Mexico, and how very choice and expensive I knew this particular American crystal was, how grateful I was to her for teaching me about quality and beauty and simplicity. I cried about the hard parts of being an American in England and how easy it is to feel rejected by a whole culture even if you know you are cherished by the English man you love. I cried and cried.

And I thought of all the things I would want to say to Christopher about this, wanting him to know how crushed I was by his moving the vase, how thoughtless I thought it was, how unaware of the symbolism of rejection in the act, how anti-American, too.

But I knew also that that kind of rage gets nobody anywhere. It only creates more hurt. It also leaves wounds that need time to heal and, in our case, causes withdrawal. Living with someone who has withdrawn and waiting for them to return while the accusations sort themselves out and connection slowly re-emerges is 100 per cent not my forte. Waiting for anything – dessert, downloads, Christmas – is hard enough. But waiting in emotional silence for healing to happen and for joy and affection to return is torment.

So on that Saturday, still holding the vase to my heart, I checked my assumptions.

Question: 'What am I assuming here that is making me so sad and angry?'

Answer: I am assuming that Christopher does not like the vase. I am assuming that he does not want any American object to be prominently displayed in our English house. I am assuming that he cares more about his own cultural preferences than about the whole 300-year history of American craftsmanship and crystal and about the whole 39-year history of my emotional relationship with my mother. I am assuming that he will never agree to have the vase out again and, unable to do anything about that, I will be a side-lined victim in my own home for the rest of my life. I am assuming, therefore, that my long-dreamed-of marital happiness as I have known it for several years is now over.

> Choosing does not mean surrender. It signals discernment.

The vase in the cupboard, it seemed, signalled the end of my personal power and my dream of a marriage.

No wonder I was a rocking-back-and-forth maniac.

Seductive as it was to stay mired (isn't it always – what is that about?), I slowly examined those assumptions one by one.

Were they true? No. Not one.

Should I base my next actions on a single one of them? Absolutely not.

Then what should determine my next actions?

The truth.

So I looked squarely at what the truth was for each of those assumptions and I put them all together into this question:

If I knew deep down without question that Christopher loves the best of America, is more interested in resolving things so that we are both happy than he is in insisting on his British preferences, that he hates for me to be unhappy, that he loved my mother and honours my relationship with her, that nothing in the world can strip me of my personal power or ability to find a good outcome in the face of disagreement and that, therefore, my happy marriage and my fulfilling life are mine after all, how would I approach Christopher about the vase?

(That is probably the longest Incisive Question on record, but in emergencies like this when you have to be your own Thinking Partner, sometimes you just have to cram everything in.)

The answer was: 'I would wait until Thursday.'

On Thursday I would raise the issue. I would know by then how to talk about it so that it reflected the whole of me, not just the sad parts, and after I had had lots of wonderful connection with him. After my big perspective on the world had returned. And, most important, with the truth as my starting point.

I did that. And here is the truly amazing, oh-so-short dialogue we had. He was drying a skillet. I walked through the kitchen and said, my heart beating a bit fast, 'Darling, you know that Steuben vase of my mother's...?'

'Yes,' he said tenderly, 'where would you like us to put it?'

'Um,' I said, disoriented by the ease of this.

'I wasn't sure it was safe in the conservatory,' he said, putting the skillet away, 'but I didn't know where you might want it. Where would you like it?'

Well, you know, it really didn't matter to me at that moment exactly where we put the beautiful damn thing; I was just so happy and so impressed by how easily this issue had resolved, and I was shuddering thinking about the blistering, badly aimed, bodies-on-the-floor of a thing it could have been had I let loose on Saturday with my accusations and rage. My untrue assumptions would have been the generator of that mess. And that would have been, as it turned out, painful and a serious waste of time.

> A relationship is not always nurtured by instant reactions.

I had chosen that battle, yes, but *after* I had lived until Thursday with the reality of the true freeing assumptions, letting the untrue ones dry up and drop off. And look how easily the 'battle' had turned into dialogue.

Since then 'waiting until Thursday' has become for me a metaphor for judiciousness, for seeding a good life by preferring the good outcome to the much-hyped so-called emotional honesty, when that honesty is fuelled by untrue assumptions.

If it is Wednesday, of course, Thursday is a little soon. But the waiting is the point, so that choosing can be intelligent. And counting to ten doesn't really do it.

The chance to choose your battles wisely by giving yourself the gift of perspective and truth before you fight is one of the kindest things you can do for yourself, and for the people you love, and even for the people and causes for which you will – fiercely, unrelentingly, heroically, thoughtfully, successfully – fight.

# Dear Meghan
# Eight

## The Amy Question

Your mother is amazing. Both of us know that. And I'd guess that if we each wrote a book about her, we would choose similar stories of her heroism, her wisdom, her endurance, her faithful relationship with love as the core of all life, her better-than-chocolate-itself humour, her sparkle and her coherently good life as a woman. And, of course, her beauty.

But there is one amazing thing about her you might not know, something for which she is now a bit famous; and I would like to tell you about it. I would also like to suggest that you follow my lead in following hers.

As a young woman, not much older than you are now, she understood about something profound. She knew that denial, the act of assuming that something is not true that is (or that something that is true is not) is dangerous. She also understood that much heartache, much disappointment, much expense, much work could be prevented if denial could be skewered.

In the years when she was Director of Admissions at our school, we used to take a walk during our lunch break. Those were the heady days in Washington of keen female political awareness of the ways in which minute-to-minute internalized sexism licks at our self-confidence, eroding slowly but surely our commitment to ourselves to be honest, clear-thinking and self-preserving, and in particular not to delude ourselves about anything.

We decided that we would take these lovely 'thinking' walks and each take a turn to answer three questions. The other would listen beautifully. Each turn would take about 20 minutes.

The three questions were:

If you were to accept no limits to your power or joy, what would you do over the next few days?

What might stop you from doing that?

How are you going to defy that limit?

These were wonderful walks. Both of us stayed on track with our lives and dreams in those days in impressive ways.

But one day, as we were dodging a low branch on the edge of the soccer field, she threw me with her question. I had said I wanted to decide whether to hire a particular candidate for a job.

'When you think about this person,' she said, 'what do you know now that you are going to find out in a year?' She asked me that question as if were just hello, how are you?

> What do you know now that you are going to find out in a year?

'What?' I asked, trying to sound offhand, losing my balance fast.

Free of the branch, she said, 'You know, when you think about him and the difficulties that could lie ahead, what do you know now that you are going to find out in a year?'

I knew. And I instantly stopped knowing.

'I don't get it,' I lied, the way you do when you definitely get it. (Lying, especially to yourself, is not uncommon when denial is on the chopping block. Denial, especially in its death throes, pads out its fabrication quotient like mad.)

'Well,' she said to me, 'face it. You usually know right away what you should do about things, but you sometimes refuse to see the problems you have already seen. I have noticed that it takes about a year for your wishful thinking to melt down.

'So I just wonder,' she went on, again as if this were not about to be a permanently formative moment of my life, 'what you are right now denying that you are going to find out in about a year when it is so in your face you have to face it? It doesn't mean you can't hire the guy. It just means that you can head off the problems now. But if you pretend they don't exist, you'll have to deal with them, as well as your disillusionment, later. And that will be a drag.'

> People deny rather than face what is right in front of them because they assume they cannot handle what will happen if they do.

I searched for sarcasm, but the nail-on-the-head wisdom of all of that full-nelsoned my tongue. And in the silence I started to think.

The answers to the question rushed under the gate, as soon as I stepped back.

I hired the man, but with my eyes (and his) wide open.

What do you know now that you are going to find out in a year? I never forgot it. I teach it now. I named it 'the Amy Question'. It has become a stabilizing element in my life. Every time I have faced now 'what I am going to find out in a year', I have been glad. Hundreds of people and many organizations now refer to the Amy Question, improving their thinking, their decisions and their lives because of it.

Over the years I have realized that people deny rather than face what is right in front of them because they assume they cannot handle what will happen if they do. So occasionally I word the Amy Question this way:

If you knew that you can handle the answer, what would you know now that you are going to find out in a year?

I don't know, Meghan, what you may be denying today. I don't know what might be right in your face that you are not facing.

It may be that there is someone hurting you, but you love or need them so much you are choosing to pretend that everything is all right. You may even be choosing to see yourself as deserving whatever they are doing to you. You may be unable even to tell that the hurt is hurting.

Or it may be that you have a cherished dream for your life that you don't dare acknowledge for fear people will trample it before it takes root.

Or it may be that you are just not asking questions about the things that seem wrong to you. Lots of people do this. They do it as Boards of Directors, as employees, as politicians, as doctors, as high priests, as parents. They do it to keep a fanciful, lucrative version of reality alive while conflicting, harder versions slowly strip the life from our society. They glimpse, register, wince, then ask no questions.

This is denial, too. Christopher recognized denial's hidden message in this injunction:

'Don't ask and don't tell. Since it didn't happen, there is nothing to discuss.'

He is right; that is exactly how denial works.

So what I hope you will do is exactly the opposite of that.

Do ask. Do tell. It is happening, and there is everything to discuss.

You can begin with the Amy Question. And let those answers lead to other questions.

You can ask why our society peddles winning. And when people tell you competition is good for people, tell them about your friends who, because they lost, can't see how good they are any more. Ask until they discuss it.

You can ask why most people on the planet are poor, and when they tell you that it is because the rich work harder, tell them that your poor friends work just as hard, harder even. Ask until they discuss it.

You can ask what your friend's aunt died of. When they tell you it was an infection, you can tell them that you saw her face just after her husband died three days before her, and you think she died of a heartbreak. Ask if they know how to cure a heartbreak.

You can ask why the law lets a grown-up hit a child but not another grown-up. When they tell you it is a grown-up's right and it is for the child's own good, ask them why it isn't good for the grown-up to be hit, too. Ask them about the strong hurting the weak. Ask until they discuss it.

You can ask why it is right to kill people to prove that killing people is wrong.

You can ask why we, masters of unparalleled intelligence, are willing to rape mountains, gut the earth and kill our seas and ourselves, just to make electricity. When they tell you it is efficient, ask them if there honestly, really and truly, is no other way to do it. Really and truly.

You can ask why people hate wrinkles. When they tell you wrinkles are ugly because old is ugly, ask them who would lose money if old became beautiful.

And before your exams if you say you are scared, and they say no you're not, you can say yes I am. You can say yes I am, until they stop saying no you're not. Then you can ask them how anyone but you, and only you, can know how you feel.

When you touch something and it burns, scream. When it is silky, coo. And when it sings back to you, fill the air with your song.

And most of all, when you wonder, you can ask. Ask and ask and ask. And then face the answers. You can notice the good in life that peeks through that question:

What do you know now that you are going to find out in a year?

There is nothing so good as reality. Nothing so relieving as truth.

# Dear Meghan
# Nine

## Interruption

There is one thing you can do right this minute. If you do it, you will automatically build a good life. And the great thing about being a woman is that we get to do this thing and not risk our womanhood. Men, on the other hand, when they do it, are seen by their culture as not real men. This is deeply stupid. But then most cultural injunctions are.

> You can decide today not to interrupt anyone ever again.

This thing is this. You can decide today not to interrupt anyone ever again (unless there is a fire). And you can ask everyone in your life to do this thing for you, too. That's it: you don't interrupt and they don't either.

Of course, you have to agree between you to be equals and not dominate or hog the conversation, and not to go on and on. To know you won't be interrupted (which is ineffable bliss) requires you to be brief and equal in your 'turns'. But that is just civilized behaviour anyway, however rare.

What I meant about the advantage of being a woman on this issue is that our culture says that 'real women' listen. Because listening is a soft thing. Men's culture says that 'real men' talk. Because talking is a strong thing. And if a man is not strong, oops, he is not a man after all. I know this is rubbish. And that we are in the lifelong business of binning it. But in the meantime we can also be pleased that we have been allowed as women to get good at one of the strongest forces in the universe: the power to generate brilliant thinking by deciding to listen. Without interruption.

Oh, and being listened to without interruption also creates the knowledge that we matter, and that seems to generate immunity hormones that help us heal and brain hormones that help us think. So says science, at the moment anyway.

How good is that?

# Dear Meghan
## Ten

### Staying Surprise-able

'At his sister's funeral,' my friend said, 'Thomas anguished more about his awkward parking space than he did about his dead sister.

'He was dry as straw,' Tenniel went on, 'bent, brittle, with nowhere to go. No juice. No questions.

'Unable,' he said, 'to be surprised.'

Ah, I thought, another component of a good life: the ability to be surprised.

Tenniel said it well. It does matter that we stay able to be surprised, to be startled, wide-eyed, grateful to realize again that every moment is new and without definition or template, and can suddenly peek around the corner out of nowhere, winking at us, beckoning, with no map and no promise of return.

Becoming juice-less like Thomas is a slow erosion, driven by the decision to see the new moment as the old, to see in it only what we have seen before, lopping off whole lumps of its unique self until it fits into us, crammed, suffocating, barren. This act desiccates the life in us because our brains and hearts were designed to welcome the new second, not to mould it into the old.

> She stayed surprise-able.

To be able to be surprised is juicy. It is a kind of passion. It indicates that we are whole and grounded, but also open, receptive and ready for the particular love-making that takes place between the present and the future, between the known and the brand new, and thus between ourselves reiterated and ourselves discovered.

I guess it would not be a bad thing if someone carved your epitaph as:

SHE STAYED SURPRISE-ABLE

# Dear Meghan
## Eleven

### Your Star

When we love another person, we get to reach all the way to the happiness we already imagine; to dress in all the lights that that place scatters across its skies. We don't have to let the cynics jade us, nor the cautious suppress us. And we don't have to let Hallmark dumb down our original take on this most ancient and intricate of adventures. Love is both complex and simple, as is the universe. When we love, we get to request its entirety.

For all its challenges, love can be as good, as deep, as respectful, as joyous, as passionate, as faithful and as grounded as we long for it to be.

I wonder what your journey there will be. Will you be cherished immediately and forever? Will you be hurt often? Will you leap too soon with no visibility and have to climb over the briars below and up the sides of granite to find a less foggy launch somewhere else and, spotting your new beloved's wing tip, know it was worth the fall and the climb? Or will you love eternally soon, and find yourself in candlelight with the same person after 65 years and after way more than most of your life?

I cannot know. Nor can you. We have only the present, and all we can do is live it so well, so truly, that our favourite future is not thwarted in its figuring out of itself.

Piloting this life of love requires ruthless honesty with yourself and with your love. It requires logic and emotional clarity and patience and the ability to distinguish the present moment from each that has gone before. These are big requirements, and you are already finding your way to them.

But for your journey I offer you an instrument of a different kind: your star. Not the kind of star whose light has travelled from so far away for so many years that it may have died while its light was finding your eyes, so that when you gaze at it you realize that what you are seeing may no longer exist. (Isn't that a staggering thought?)

The kind of star I am talking about, this navigating instrument for love, is different. It is alive. It exists inside you. It needs no time or journey to get to you. Maybe it is act one of intuition. Or maybe it is a particularly language-less and stunningly accurate voice of some eternal entity. It doesn't matter what it is. It matters that it is. Because it is just about the most trustworthy guide you will ever invoke. Its light is beaming toward only one thing: your good life.

> That is what your star does. It out-imagines you.

All you have to do to see it is to be still. Then look. At nothing. See the answer in a hand-brush of colour, in a confident settling-in, in all the congregating multiple nods and breathings and embraces that make up the knowledge inside a human being that what is being sensed is true.

I said language-less. It certainly is. It is nearly impossible to find words for it. And when it shines or speaks, it does so with swirlings and leanings, in textures and echoes, in a gentle gathering of gravity between you and it, in that synapse of something that makes you smile from knowing.

When Christopher and I met, all of that happened for me all at once. My knees went weak and I had to sit down, confusing many closed-minded feminists who were watching as he and I walked across the room toward each other. I know it sounds very *South Pacific*. And I can tell you all the sweet details of that evening if you want sometime.

But the reason I mention that weak-knees first few minutes of knowing Christopher is that I was certain beyond anything that he and I were meant to love each other forever, but there was not one rational, objective, plan-worthy, here-take-this-route hint that we could possibly be together. And the concept of marriage as an eventual expression of this love was out of the question. Objectively speaking.

But I knew. And he told me 24 hours later that he knew, too. Not in detail back then. But we knew that what had happened to us was undeniable, powerful and, in some life-forming sense, not to be resisted.

We knew, but there was no reason to know. There was every logical reason to rebuff the knowing. And as the days went by and turned into happier and more certain knowing, and into months, Christopher asked a friend, another rational, high-achieving, romantic-but-not-sentimental activist, how to describe this phenomenon of knowing that love is right but not knowing where it can lead. 'Follow your star,' his friend said, sentimentality making sense.

We did as he said. And the path has been both divinely unpredictable, giving us riches of meaning and fulfilment unplottable 32 years ago, and also sweetly traditional, giving us marriage and a home together and the irreplaceable thing of being each other's family.

That is what your star does. It out-imagines you. It illuminates the good in your life. It blesses you with the rewards that come from trusting the sight of the thing you cannot see.

# Dear Meghan
## Twelve

### Somethings

Driving into London recently I was listening to BBC Radio 4 (reason in itself to move to England, the first being love, another the NHS). The programme was an interview with the author of a book whose thesis is that life is divided into two experiences: 'Somethings' and 'Nothings'.

Somethings he defines as 'locally financed and produced, and having wholly unique characteristics': Aldermaston bowls, JayPen calligraphy and Pierreponts Café of Goring-on-Thames. Nothings he defines as 'centrally financed and produced, having no unique characteristics': Corelle dinnerware, Skype text fonts and Pizza Hut.

He says that Somethings are a result of independent thinking. They keep us smart, sensitive and creative. They require us to think, and to respond in complex and enlightened ways. They engage us. Nothings, on the other hand, are a result of derivative thinking. They deplete us, require nothing of us and dull our thinking and our sensitivities.

The surprising aspect of these two life options, according to this author, is that they are not based on wealth or status. The rich and powerful are just as likely to be seduced by Nothings and to pay small fortunes for Nothings as unknown people on a budget. The danger we face, he says, is in Nothings' ever-present allure through convenience and fashion and in the idea that the high price or convenience of Nothings indicates the presence of Somethings.

Consciously to select Somethings is to resist seduction and to select our human heritage of thinking, growing, considering and delving – of daring to be ourselves.

The point here is not to be a snob, but rather to decide to go for quality even when we have only disappearing amounts of money to spend. The point is to decide that when possible we will give a little more time to finding one truly beautifully made, distinctive garment, instead of eight over-in-an-instant-on-sale, centrally controlled and made, undistinctive pieces for the same money. A Something is a treasure, both because it is exquisitely made and because it will be stunning for the whole of its life.

We can do the same with food. We can find or prepare beautifully created, meaningfully conceived food and take time with each bite. Sometimes this food will be more expensive, but not always. As with all Somethings, the food comes from original thinking, from real hands and real hearts rather than from the alienated anonymity of the corporate thinking-for-you centre. The cost of it is not always the clue to the nature of it.

> Things of quality sing to us, and we are grounded as we listen.

We can do the same also with vessels. We can seek the real, the handmade, the specially-thought-about, the impossible-to-perfect.

The same is true with furniture. It can be full of story because it is old or one-of-a-kind or because it survived tragedy or celebrated love. Some of it may be made by someone you know, full of lovely lines and internal strength or breathtaking delicacy.

Things of quality sing to us, and we are comforted, inspired and grounded as we listen. Each time you look at your Somethings, or wear them, or remember the taste or sound or texture of them, or go back through the photos of them, you will feel a surge of self-respect. Somethings say back to you that you, too, are distinctive. This reminder will give you physical energy, as my friend Bill Ford teaches, the way all experiences of self-respect do.

And so, I encourage you to choose Somethings as often as possible. To save for them when they are expensive. To go out of your way for them even when they cost hardly anything. And then to take care of them because they are priceless.

This is not difficult to suggest to you, Meghan, because you seem inherently to seek Somethings in most of what you do and buy and experience. You care about the beginnings of things. You may enjoy the trend, but you embrace passionately the original. And you like to feel your mind at work, your sensitivities charged. You reach for the heart of things. You cherish the authentic.

I whisper to you today my father's highest compliment, which now, in the context of this theory, holds new meaning for me. And I offer it to you with my dad's deep and tender Tennessee voice alive in my ear:

'Honey, you are something.'

# Dear Meghan
## Thirteen

### Joy

It is perverse, but our society seems to think that what is real is what is bad. What is good and lovely and positive and successful is regarded as not real somehow. I run into this travesty a lot. You probably do, too. People say things like:

Let's get real here. (Let's admit what is bad.)

Would you like some honest feedback? (Would you like to know how badly you did?)

The truth is…. (What is bad is….)

If we spend too much time feeling good, reality (bad stuff) will sideswipe us.

But the truth is that reality is not just what is bad. It is also what is good. To interpret reality as being only the bad, and the good as being a dismissible, or even dangerous, diversion, is to be wrong much of the time. And so it leads you to make decisions in a state of inaccuracy.

To make the best decisions, you have to factor in all of reality. And that includes the good. To be accurate about things, you have to see and articulate the successes, the positive leaning, the light-imbued side of the issue. Otherwise, you create a distorted next step. So in the name of accuracy you can begin with, and weave in, what is good as you tackle what is bad.

In all of this balancing of bad with good, how you feel about your world is also at stake. Over this you have say every minute, even in the face of the worst of the bad. Your feelings spring from assumptions. And among the core, true assumptions you can decide to make at any moment are:

You are good.
You have choice in this moment.
It is all right to feel happy even if others in the world are sad.
Things can turn out better than you can imagine.

The circumstances may be grim: we may be at war; there may be only four seal otters left on the planet; pay differentials may be 300 to 1; chickens may be handing human beings a plague of killer flu; high antibiotic resistance may be making our hospitals more dangerous than city streets; school systems may be testing children at younger and younger ages, thus snuffing their early love for learning; you may have just been lied to and betrayed, or you may be facing memory loss or job loss or bone loss.

> It is all right to feel happy even if others in the world are sad.

And yet, in this exact second, you are fine. You do not have a hair dryer in your bath water or a brute on your body or a crawl space full of rats devouring your brain. You are okay. And so you have choice about how widely and hopefully you relate to your world.

In fact, even in life-threatening moments, you have options. You have options even about what assumptions to make and thus about how you can begin to feel. And of course how you feel right this second determines how you handle the next second, from what perspective you make the decision to do the next thing. (How you feel also probably helps create the reality you experience. But that is another book.)

## Choose joy, having considered all the facts.

Oh, and don't ever forget how this may tie in with immunity. According to the biochemist Lydia Temoshok, immune cells reproduce in just the right amount and proportion when joy is their dependable environment. Immunity needs a focus on the truly good – how important is that?

So consider today that good is real. You do not have to worry about being sabotaged by 'reality'.

From an anonymous poem this advice first touched me. I offer it to you now as you journey through womanhood:

Choose joy, having considered all the facts.

It is an informed, intelligent, nimble, necessary way to a good life.

# Hattie

Given that we all die, how do
we find meaning in living?

# Dear Hattie

## Introduction

### The Meaning of Meaning

People talk about the meaning of life as if everyone knows what it is. This is silly. Meaning is elusive. We are forever searching for it. To find it we have to think about it. No one can tell us what it is. We have to figure out what it is for us. Only then can we translate that vast abstraction into real things, things we promise and pursue.

Your question is articulate and profound: 'Given that we all die, how do we find meaning in living?' You are in good company. Viktor Frankl wondered about this, too. His masterpiece *Man's Search for Meaning* (I hope it will become one of your treasures) questions meaning in the context of death, as you do. We could do well to start with his ideas.

> Meaning emerges each time we do Human Being as exquisitely as we can.

But perhaps your question's answers will emerge best from the question behind it: 'Does death negate the meaning of life?'

Does a life that is short – even 99 years is a short life when compared with the length of time we are dead – have less meaning than a life that is forever? How long would a person or thing have to live in order for that life to have meaning? Does a human infant, born at noon but dead by dusk, have a meaningless life; and did that infant, and did we, experience no meaning in that life? If so, how long would she have had to live in order for her existence to have become meaningful? Seven days? Ten years? A hundred and nine? Does length of life determine meaning of life?

Does the fact that a particular dragonfly, indisputably one of the most elegant creatures on earth, can die within only two weeks of being a free-flying adult, strip meaning from its living? In the moment you see it, would you rather it had not lived just because it may not last the night? Would you wish never to have taken in the lustre on its layered wings or the tickling as it hovers?

The meaning in the dragonfly's life, for us anyway, is in its just being completely and wholly what it is, doing Dragonfly as exquisitely as it can, and bestowing on our moments and our memories that beauty and that particular goodness.

Maybe human life is the same. Although our genes code us to live 130 years, we could, like the dragonfly, die today. Perhaps we should explore, then, what it would take to be completely and wholly who we are, to grace each other's moments and memories with our beauty and with our particular goodness.

And so, I wonder, could it be that, even in the face of the inevitability of death, meaning emerges each time we do Human Being as exquisitely as we can?

# Dear Hattie

## One

### Before They Die

Think of two people you love. If they were suddenly to die tonight, what words of respect would you wish you had said to them today?

Although you have no doubt imagined and feared these people's death (we all do, and most certainly you imagined Fred's), you cannot possibly know what it would be like if they were to leave forever. And because you cannot know that, you don't have a preview of that cavern of regret that will overtake you if, suddenly without them, you realize that you did not say the things you feel deep down. The trouble with a person's dying is that you can't say it to them afterward. It is not like they're going off to a new job or even to Tierra del Fuego.

> The thing we know for sure is that we don't know how long we have.

After their death you can't call them up. You can talk to their spirit and hope that it exists and that it hears. But to be sure they know, you have to say it now. Now, because the thing we know for sure is that we don't know how long we have.

The regret of having not said the things we love about people dear to us is almost inconsolable. It is worse in some ways even than the pain of losing them. I think this pain speaks of an inherent need to love and to express our loving. Not to express it is a freezing of something vital. At some level we know this, and at some level we plan to say the loving things someday. The freezing is temporary, we think, and so does not actively ache.

But when death comes before we get around to saying those loving things, the freezing is fast and hard, and it hurts. We can forgive ourselves eventually, but the thaw never quite completes.

Our society has a lot to answer for here. Its injunction not to say how much we love each other, not to express admiration, appreciation, respect, but rather to joke or dismiss or criticize, is the real architect of most anxious moments and many failed lives. If people were told several times a day in several different ways, explicitly, what they mean to people, how they are valued, what they have done well, almost everything in their day and their accumulated days would be stronger, smarter, more a song.

Carl Rogers, whose thinking I recommend to you, had a very interesting take on this. He said that we are born with self-regard, knowing we are good and full of positive potential. We love ourselves and are wired to love others, without conditions. But the grown-ups in our life tell us that to be loved and lovable we have to do and think and be certain things. We learn what he calls 'conditions of worth'. Those conditions don't fit with our inborn sense of ourselves as fine and inherently good. And the resulting 'incongruence' produces anxiety, depression and even violent behaviour. Not telling people what you love and admire about them, then, is more than just an oversight. It is a collision of plates deep beneath the surface of a life.

It is assumed that if we tell people what we treasure about them, they will become intellectually undiscerning and disappear into a kind of mush of narcissism. We certainly assume that something not good will happen, and that it is safer and wiser to hold back the words of love.

The trouble with this is that we do love each other. We love each other so much we can hardly stand it. Our love, our regard for each other, our cherishing of each other is so big and so basic and so active we have to contort in order not to say it. We have to twist our fine impulses into hemp in order not to say things, cry things, hug and hold each other and laugh from the sheer ecstasy of noticing each other. Our love for each other is in us. It is in those mysterious places between places, in the space that defines the substance. It makes us. And to deny it is in itself a kind of dying.

So, consider this: even in the middle of your adolescence when being cool is in fact being cool, when nearly four-fifths of a century still stretches out before you and final endings seem silly and remote, write down what you treasure about Fred, and about Ollie, about your mother and your dad and anyone else you love. Then tell them. Today. And don't let them put you off. Make them listen. Tell them that the appropriate response is a simple 'thank you'. No rebuttal.

You can then let some of those messages become just the way your day is, day after day. Let your culture of being be the expression of love, the noticing and saying what is good in people. Let the arguments and criticisms, even the looks of criticism, be rare. Let the expression of love and respect be the norm.

You can do this because it will best express who you are. And in doing so it will bring meaning to those moments.

You can do it also so that when the people you love leave forever, peace, not remorse, will be the nucleus of the pain. As the pain subsides and changes to acceptance and you fashion a new life, your heart will still hear theirs, unencumbered.

# Dear Hattie

## Two

### You Choose

Others still control much of your life. They will for a few more years. Until you can pay, you obey. Such is childhood. And where you are now is the skin-shedding between child and adult. It seems to take forever, and it smarts because the familiar rips as it goes. This period can also seem punctuated by betrayal, as adults' best efforts wobble and pedestals topple.

But the only real betrayal here is society's slow installation of the assumption that we do not have choice. Meaning in life can be chewed up by that assumption. 'I am trapped' is probably not an exquisite doing of Human Being.

Choice, however, is. This phenomenon of choice pertains not just to what you do, or with whom you do it. It pertains also to how you feel and, most important, how you feel about yourself. You can choose to think well of yourself, deep down, all of the time. Meaning springs from there.

I remember Ingrid. That afternoon she was playing the piano in our music corner. Schubert, I think. I sat down on the chair nearby. I listened.

I knew her playing. She was gifted. That day, though, the notes seemed to come not from her usual reservoir, but from the piecing together of something pushed away.

She looked up. I smiled. She tried to smile back. She bowed her head and then tossed it back, her hair sweeping almost in slow motion past her cheeks and into a split-second sail behind her. She closed her eyes. I knew she was deciding not to cry, forcing the already-rushing pulses back. Her hands left the keyboard.

'What is it?' I whispered.

She shook her head. She stopped stopping the tears. I rose from my chair slowly and moved to the piano bench.

'Can you tell me?'

'Probably not,' she said after a few seconds.

'If you could, would you?' I said, still softly. I sat.

'Yes.'

I waited.

'Is it ever the right thing to do to do the wrong thing?' she asked, still not looking up.

I was quiet. This was not a question to be answered, only respected.

She spoke. 'Sometimes you have to choose between yourself and other people. Their feelings, I mean. You choose them. But then you snap. You realize that you can't any more. But then suddenly you aren't choosing yourself or them because it is too late.'

I remained quiet.

'We've been chem lab partners. I guess parties are different from classes. Obviously. But what I mean is that parties change people. Drinking, too. They were not the same. Ben most of all.'

Her right hand lifted. C above high C. Then C. Then nothing.

'I left, with them. The library seemed okay to me. We were laughing. No research tonight. Ha ha. Then Lex closed the tall doors and locked them. I wondered about that. But I had had a drink, too. And we were laughing.

'Then Ben reached out to hug me. I let him and sort of hugged him back. It was weird because we had only ever done chem reports together. But I just let it happen. It seemed sweet.

'Then he pulled away a tiny bit and he put his hand behind my neck and shoved his tongue into my mouth. He pulled my shirt down over my shoulder.

'Everything from then on seems like someone else's life.'

I still did not move. Ingrid was quiet.

'Anyway,' she continued slowly, 'it got worse. And Adam and Lex didn't stop him even when I screamed for him to stop. Why didn't they do something? How did I let that happen? What is wrong with me?'

I listened.

'Who am I now?' she said hardly audible. She closed the keyboard lid.

'I should go,' she said. She stood.

'Do you have a class?' I asked.

'No, but I don't feel very good.'

'If you talk a little more,' I said gently, 'maybe you will feel better.'

'I don't think so. This is about me, and that can't change. That is what I am. And I am sure they think that.

'How can I sit at the bench with them tomorrow? There is now this monster between us. And I don't mean just Ben. Me, too. I should never have gone out with them, and I shouldn't have had a drink, and I certainly should not have hugged Ben in that first second. I should have done something the minute Lex locked the door. I wondered about it, but I didn't do anything. I didn't want to insult them.

You can choose to think well of yourself, deep down, all of the time.

'The thing is, what does all of that make me?' She sat.

I ventured a perspective, gently. 'Do you think that who we are deep inside is changed by what people do to us?'

'I don't know who I am deep inside. I thought I did. But now I don't.'

'Who did you think you were before last night?'

'Oh, well, maybe I thought my mom might be right, that I am good. That would be nice. But now I seriously think she was wrong.'

She was slipping fast into choicelessness, into that vortical message of society that says that women are bad if men do bad things to us.

This is played out, as you probably know, in chilling ways. Sometimes women are stoned for having sex outside of their marriage. The men in the liaisons are not punished. And you can still hear rape described as being caused by a woman's seductive clothing or alluring behaviour, as if the man had no brain.

But I could not, of course, say all of this. She needed the core truth. The rest would follow.

I asked slowly, 'If you knew, Ingrid, that you can choose to see that you are wholly good, what would you feel?'

She looked at me and was quiet.

'That is an amazing question,' she said. 'I don't know.'

I nodded.

'I need to think about it,' she said. 'For a split second, I felt better. But I am not sure now. What was the question?'

She opened the keyboard lid. She placed both hands on the keys and spread her fingers.

I asked again.

After a while she said, 'I can choose. I am thinking about that.' She looked across into places beyond this corner.

'Maybe I am not theirs,' she said.

She returned to Schubert.

Ingrid's introduction to choice was a private one. But choice is also what the most successful fighters of oppression have known in their hearts. The choices they made led to freedom. In the very pit of prejudice Mary Anning found the Ichthyosaurus, Martin Luther King catalysed a dream, Harriet Tubman followed the North Star, Nelson Mandela planned from prison, George Fox climbed Pendle Hill, George Eliot wrote *Middlemarch*. They chose to see their core. And to keep seeing it.

## We can choose.
## We are not theirs.

They lived this question:

If I knew that I have choice, how would I behave in this moment?

It is probably true to say that we have meaning in our lives proportionate to the decreasing amount of time each day we spend as victims.

Ingrid was right. We can choose.

We are not theirs.

# Dear Hattie

## Three

## If It Doesn't Make You Dance...

My friend Bill Ford made a wonderful discovery. He found that some surprising things give you physical energy. Things like focusing, de-cluttering, knowing your priorities, being with people who inspire you, doing nagging tasks, simplifying, finishing things, being listened to, being appreciated. His book (*High Energy Habits*) is good. You might want to read it every year just to be sure you are up to scratch in the energy department.

My favourite of his insights is that you can test whether a decision you are about to make is right by noticing whether it gives you energy. If it does, you are probably on the right track. If it doesn't, you should probably take another turn at the drawing board.

One of my clients is on the cusp of her career. She has a law degree. She worked hard for it. She used to say that she might as well have had twins for all the sleep she was getting during those graduate years. She passed with honours. Everyone was proud.

And that was the problem. As they celebrated her degree with one glass of champagne, they scoped out for her with another what she should be doing for the next 30 years. The conversations elided, and collided, inside her.

'It's strange,' she said to me. 'I can feel energy leave my body every time I hear other people's pictures of my upcoming glorious life as an attorney. Nothing about it appeals to me. If I am honest, I think I just wanted to prove to myself, and to a few particular sceptics, that I could graduate from law school with honours. I concentrated on that the whole time. I didn't go to law school with a lawyer's life in mind.

'And at these celebrations people jerk my future around, and I just stand there, smiling. No one knows what they stir up inside me. I wish we could have celebrated without moving on so fast.'

Anna was right. When we have achieved something that is big for us, whatever it is, we deserve to be feted without having to discuss next steps. Questions at congratulations parties should probably be, 'How did you do it? What was hardest? What are you most proud of? Did you ever feel like giving up? What kept you going? What did you most enjoy about it?' A celebration should be a time of reflection on the achievement, period.

But the thing that really caught my ear and concerned me was her reference to losing energy – an almost certain sign that being a lawyer was not the right direction for her life. Energy betrays our most careful efforts to seem fine. Energy is a remarkably dependable clue as to whether we should walk in a particular direction, or stop right there and draw a new map with destinations and roads that make us jump around and definitely want to get up in the morning.

> It is meaning that makes you dance.

So I asked her, 'Anna, when you think about what you want to do with your life for the next 30 years, what ideas give you energy?'

This is a very different question from: 'What would success look like for you?' Or, 'What do you want to be able to say about your life just before you die?' Or, 'How can you use your best talents to earn a good living?' Or even, 'What could you do that would make you happy?'

Energy is a unique focus, and its questions often reveal unexpected, even heretical, answers.

'Well, not trying court cases, or drawing up contracts or wills, or mediating litigants, or defending corporations. I can definitely tell you that.'

'And what would give you energy?'

'Good question. And I know the answer. But nobody is going to like it. I mean, how do parents feel when their child spends thousands of their dollars for a degree with a clear and lucrative direction implied, and then lowers the sails, jumps and swims out of view? How would that provide a return on their investment, as my dad would, will, say?'

'So what is this heresy that would give you energy?' I persisted.

'A collage,' she said. 'Several things at once. And that is just not acceptable. I am now a master-in-the-making of one trade. That is where respect lies.'

'And what is it, this collage?'

She smiled. Already the energy was creeping back into her face.

'Researching social policy, restoring ancient manuscripts and playing the organ.' She leaned over closer to me. 'Doesn't that sound fabulous?'

The thing, of course, about helping someone think for themselves is that you have to be pretty sharp about which questions are to be answered literally and which are not. I knew unequivocally that this was a do-not-answer question.

I knew this for two reasons: first, because what mattered only in this moment was that she relish that answer, soak in it, with my acceptance and warmth, so that she would not tumble back into the trap of pleasing the authority figures in her life; and second, because I personally could not think of three things that would suck the energy right out my body faster than researching social policy, restoring ancient manuscripts and playing the organ.

So I smiled and kept listening.

'The problem is, of course,' she went on, 'that that collage has nothing to do with law. And I have no idea at all how I would make a living doing those things. But, oh, they make me want to dance.'

She paused. 'What do you think?' she asked me. She clearly wanted an answer this time.

'You know,' I said, 'when my mother and I went shopping together, she used to say as I tried on each outfit, "If it doesn't make you dance, don't buy it." She was wise. I nearly always pushed further and further into the back of the closet the things that hadn't made me dance in the dressing room.'

Anna smiled. 'How about this for a career-planning motto: "If it doesn't make you dance, don't do it?" Because if you do it, it will, I bet, now that I think about it, be, in every sense, way too expensive in the long run.'

'And the biggest price you will pay,' I confirmed, 'will be energy, and then health, and then your life. That's pretty big.'

Anna never looked back. Her well-trained, logical, probing lawyer's mind and just-right degree of independence served her well. She made her life her own, made a good enough living and continued most of the time to let 'Does it make me dance (does it give me energy)?' be her guide for most things. It impressed me enough to continue to research this concept.

And maybe, Hattie, you will consider Anna's juncture as you approach your own. Maybe you will notice first what lifts your heart, fills your muscles with get-up-and-go, keeps you smiling at just the thought of it and seems to say 'Hattie' on it in the bottom corner.

It is meaning that makes you dance.

# Dear Hattie
## Four

### Each Crystal Goblet

Don't worry. I know that crystal is my thing, not yours (at least not yet; godmothers always hope to pass on passions like this but shouldn't hold their breath; and it is enough for me that we both adore turquoise). I also know that crystal's relevance to finding meaning in living is zilch.

> Setting boundaries develops freedom.

But knowing how to treat crystal – that is a different thing. That matters. Meaning resides there. Master it and you have mastered one of the most important behaviours between human beings ever sussed out by psychologists. Relating successfully to crystal is an unbeatable metaphor for a far-reaching vessel of meaning: boundaries.

Boundary is a sophisticated concept. It permeates a long spectrum of relationships from lovers to political heads of state, with therapists, customers, employees, clients, parents, carers, teachers, doctors, bus drivers and friends scattered around in the middle.

Boundaries prevent invasion. That is their function. They keep us safe from uninvited guests. And they keep our self in full view. Boundaries, because they protect us from emotional burglaries, invasions and take-overs, also build good relationships for us. People whose boundaries have been violated and who, therefore, don't know where they end and others begin, cannot build authentic relationships. They are too busy searching for themselves in the other person.

Robert Frost knew about boundaries. In 'The Mending Wall' he concluded this way:

Good fences make good neighbours.

(Don't you love how some people can summarize whole fields of knowledge in five words?)

When you respect a person's boundaries, you respect them. In practice this means that you are clear about what you expect of each other, what your 'contract' is. In business or professional life, this is sometimes an actual contract, even a legal one.

But, as we saw with Ingrid, the concept of contract applies just as crucially to friends and to family. Boundaries tell you what the relationship does not include. So, with real friends, for example, the relationship does not usually include exclusivity; it does not include sex; it does not include borrowing large amounts of money; it does not include cheating on tests, or savaging each other with criticism. And if one of you operates as if it does include one of those things, you quickly find yourself at the end of the friendship. Crossing boundaries is that rupturing.

The relationships that get into deepest trouble when boundaries are crossed are the sacred ones, ones conceived and contracted in deep trust. Relationships with professional carers and parents are the key sacred ones. Entering these relationships you assume, without having to ask, that you will not be turned into a pawn of their pathological needs. So when they transgress that contract, you are by definition invaded.

The shocking thing about this is that the invading of sacred relationships is not unusual. You want to keep your eyes open. Although trust is usually warranted in our lives, it sometimes isn't. We need to see what is right in front of us. Some of the most nobly motivated, respected professionals are also predators. Addiction is addiction wherever it lurks. Even, as we have learned, in the dark chambers of priests.

And if the addiction is to sex or power, the addict's client, student, parishioner or patient is the perfect fix. Trust brings the client in. Trust builds a relationship. And when trust morphs into dependency, the client is likely to choose to interpret as all right the very not-all-right things that gradually begin to happen.

It might be good to think about each of your primary relationships. Make a list. What in each relationship have you agreed, implicitly and explicitly, you will do and be with each other? What have you agreed you will not do?

When you know the answers to these questions, you have clearly identified the boundaries of those relationships. Can you then confirm with each person that they assume those are the boundaries, too? Talking to people in this way is not stilted or odd. It is respectful and usually leads to deeper communication and joy.

So where, you might well ask, is the crystal in all of this? It is in the sink. There just under the bubbles in perfect-temperature soapy water is one crystal goblet. Just one. Put another one in there and the chances increase by a factor of nearly 32 (which is a lot) that one of the goblets will break. Why this should be so when all those giggly buoyant molecules seem to beckon like a feather-bed beats me. But it is virtually inevitable.

The water, the caressing boundary of the thin glass, seems, when invaded by another glass, to draw back and then force the sides of the two glasses together. It is as if the water were saying, 'Only one delicate individual can live with wholeness inside each boundary. One of you will have to break.'

I would suggest you try it, but it is an expensive experiment. Instead, you can take my word for it and let the metaphor ring in your ears and in your heart every time you consider letting another person invade you. You can turn to the image of the crystal when you find you have not negotiated clear expectations in your relationships.

And you don't have to be dissuaded from this conscious setting of boundaries by the businessy, unspontaneous-sounding nature of it. Spontaneous is wonderful. But very soon after spontaneous, clear had better kick in or spontaneous will become subsumption, and soon businessy will seem like bliss.

When Christopher and I met, we spent the first three days riveted by each other, discovering as much as we could about each other. We also asked each other questions about our expectations and about the challenges we might find in the relationship. It was a very non-businessy, intimate experience. But we were in fact clarifying our boundaries, making a contract together.

And as the months and years passed, and our relationship grew, we 'updated' those boundaries every so often. With every new level of clarity, we came closer, more deeply respectful of each other. The possibilities for our future grew also.

I think that because setting boundaries is an act of self-respect, and because true and lasting love originates in self-respect, setting boundaries develops freedom. Real freedom. The freedom to be yourself, and to love another person fully, ensuring their flourishing. And yours.

Kahlil Gibran's *The Prophet*, a favourite of my mother's, was talking about boundaries that lead to freedom in his piece about marriage:

Let there be spaces in your togetherness
And let the winds of the heavens dance between you.

Perhaps he knew something about crystal.

# Dear Hattie

## Five

### One Sentence

'What is your book going to be about?' my friend Bill Godwin asked me that evening. It was July in Maryland and we were hoping to cool off by heading for the front lawn away from the porch where most of the other hot people were, and where two beer-driven jazz singers were improvising. But Southern summers don't kid around, and night could just as well be noon except that there are more mosquitoes. Why I love it there, I don't know. Love is a funny thing, even the geographical kind.

'It's about thinking,' I said. 'About how we can help each other with that. It is about what happens when people interrupt us or put us down or tell us what to think or walk away. It is about how all of this translates to poor policies and corruption and poverty and disastrous relationships. It is about breakthroughs that happen when we listen in a certain way. It is about a particular kind of question that gets rid of blocks in people's thinking, almost like magic, but with rigour. It is about transformation through thinking for ourselves, I guess.'

I smiled. I seemed to need Bill to admire me, I think because I admired him so much. This unworked-out thing makes me simultaneously eager to hear what he really thinks and scared to death of it. I kept smiling.

'Put it into one sentence, Nancy,' he said. 'Until you can do that, you're not ready to write the book.'

I didn't say back to him, 'For goodness sake, Bill, this is just a summer party with some so-so music and pretty good enchiladas and very cool fireflies, so back off on the mentoring thing. Please like me, by the way.'

Nope, I just grew right up and said, 'Sure, I'll think about that. Thanks.'

There really is nothing else to do with brilliant, cut-it-like-a-knife guidance, unsolicited or not. If you want to kill the person, it probably means they are right on the button and you should just slip away and let it sink in and pull it out later to consider seriously when no one is looking. Just stand tall, say thank you and gingerly change the subject. Don't even ask questions to try to understand it. You understand it perfectly well. That is why you hate it.

So I did think about it and, sure enough, I really knew what my book was about only when I finally could reduce it to one sentence. Not even two. One. And of course the concept was much easier to sell to a publisher after that, too. Here was my sentence: this book explores ten ways a person can behave in order to help other people to think for themselves. That's it. The rest of the good stuff was all in there and would come out in the chapters. The book has sold 75,000 copies and is now in its 14th printing. Thanks, Bill. Great party.

Reducing things to one sentence is more than clarifying and telescoping. It is an act of originality. When you can express your view in one sentence, you will have created something; or, existentially speaking, you will have found the original. You will have arrived at your own thoughts. You will see that your ideas no longer wander and bump into other things. They stand ready. They are yours. One sentence. It can't be a very long sentence, either. None of this Cicero-422-word-three-clause-actually-it's-a-paragraph obfuscation. Nothing germinal ever takes place in those.

This applies to more than writing. It is powerful in defining who you are, too. Figuring out what your purpose is – who the original you is, why you are here, what you want to contribute, to do, to leave behind, to express – takes some time.

And there is no rush. That sentence will evolve for the rest of your life. But along the way, when you find that you can say as succinctly as that who you are, you will know that person. Meaning emerges as we pare.

## Meaning emerges as we pare.

In one sentence, who are you? Who is this completely original, never-been-here-before, exquisite soul that is you?

You see her. You notice what she – you – cares about most. You notice what makes you proud. You notice what you are good at and what you want to get better at. You notice what you feel good about when you do it. You notice what gives you energy – and, paradoxically, peace.

You notice what you would want most to notice if you were noticing you. You notice what of you you would want to take into eternity.

Without others' eyes watching or others' tongues advising, what do you find? By your age we have dependable clues. By 17 I already knew I wanted to teach ideas. I wanted to love. And I wanted to figure out how to help people to think for themselves.

If you can see glimpses of you, if you can embrace those things now, you will build a life of meaning. Notice them today, balance them in your palm and allow them to tell you how best to take them into the world.

# Dear Hattie

## Six

### The Final 10 Per Cent

Our world plays hide and seek with discipline, another source of meaning. We see it dart in and out of view. We seek it, but we rarely catch it. Our society does not want us to understand it. Discipline, doing the final 10 per cent of anything, allows us suddenly to see the world differently. If we did it all of the time, we would gradually become unwilling to tolerate the settling-for that passes for good. We would demand change, as a few, extraordinary people have over time. So there is courage in this discipline of doing the final 10 per cent. 'It is the kind of courage that counters the fear, as Marianne Williamson said, 'not that we are inadequate,' but 'that we are powerful beyond measure'.

And there is in the final 10 per cent a decision to know joy rather than just to long for it, or to deride it, in a ruthless world. Joy that comes from taking something all the way to its finest end point, rather than cutting it short and nursing disappointment, is nearly luscious, like Bolivian ferns or sun on wet skin. And most of us are told that such lusciousness is indulgent rather than deserved.

And so most of us do not do the final 10 per cent. It sits there opening its arms to us, but we walk away, eyes on it for a moment and then eyes down, drawn into the familiarity of somedays and almosts and someone elses. Not us. Not now. We must stay just shy of that joy. What would happen to the structure of our striving lives, the pawns of predatory economic and political systems, if we were to go to the end and really, really achieve the whole thing?

I noted this reluctance when I was coaching one of my favourite clients. 'I just did not quite do it,' she said. 'All I needed was to get two resource people, but I got distracted, didn't return the phone calls, and a week later ended up writing the report myself, which took all night. The next day the board decided the report did not justify the funding. I didn't have the compelling research figures. Why didn't I return those phone calls? What was so hard about that last little bit?'

> True discipline is deep engagement.

This is the 10 per cent phenomenon, I thought. We just don't do it. We don't dare to be that good.

I hope you will dare to be that good, Hattie. I hope you will recognize when you are in the final 10 per cent zone and not back away. I hope you will be willing to shine that brightly, to be a pioneer, a creative finisher, a master of lifelong relationships, to listen all the way to the end of people's thoughts, and to your own. I hope you will go all the way past good enough to brilliant. Brilliant, especially, in your own eyes.

This is real discipline. And real discipline is elegant. It is fun. It is almost too much fun, in fact. And because life is supposed to be all serious and hard and everything, we think of discipline as strict, dry, dogged, the bad part before the bliss – long before, maybe even instead of.

'How did you do it?' people ask. Discipline, you say. And they frown. Ah, yes, discipline, they say, the thing that spurns pleasure and that few can master, but out of which noble things are supposed to come even if we are bored, boring and brain dead at the end of it. Discipline. Glad you have some. But don't let it kill your sense of humour.

So goes the lazy lie. That bleak bunk has nothing to do with true discipline. If it is tedious, if it is untouchable, it is not real discipline. If it is someone else's idea of what you should be doing, it is not discipline. (That is obedience, which is definitely not meaningful.) And if it makes you yawn and count the minutes, it is not real discipline. Basically, if it is not fulfilling, exciting you with its promise, it is something else labelled as discipline by the deeply disappointed-in-themselves people who want you to give up before you shine. (It is no surprise that the definitions of discipline include both mental self-control and punishment.)

True discipline is deep engagement. Discipline is the building of love between you and your project. It is the decision to stay, to let your whole self be wholly committed, to snuggle down into the sinew of the thing and let it happen to you. Discipline is not the task or the task master. It is the masterful route to mastery.

You already know something of this. You knew it when you were creating the children's play centre and that mesmerizing zebra-and-lion print. You knew it when you raced back to your house after our summer lunch the year Bill died and made a collage of my favourite photos of him, framed it and put the twin poem he had given me on the back, and then brought it to me with the warmest smile in your eyes, making tears of gratitude and wonder in mine.

And you knew it when you were sitting with Fred ready to do whatever he needed. Those things did not feel to you like discipline because they were completely absorbing, because you wanted to do them and because they were an expression of you. But they were. They were real discipline. In each of those you did the final 10 per cent. It was from there that the smile emerged, the pride in your face, that inside knowledge that it was good.

Not everything has to be at this level, of course. Some things aren't meant to be thoroughly done or deeply experienced.

But when it comes to things that shape and define and express you, don't ever be proud of skimping or getting by. You don't have to be afraid to be really, really good, as good as you can be in that moment, on that day, in that year. You can notice when the final 10 per cent puts out its hand. And you can take it. If you let it, discipline will lead you to meaning you can't get any other way.

# Dear Hattie
## Seven

### Enough Enemies

You asked me once about Quakerism. I told you about its profound understanding of generative silence and its view that 'there is that of God in every person'. And we talked about its belief in non-violence as the way to end violence. And we mused about its other name, 'The Society of Friends'.

So you can imagine my surprise when one of the great Quaker mentors in my life said to me one day, when I was about 30, 'Nancy, you don't have enough enemies.'

I looked shocked, I am sure. He went on, 'You have values you passionately want to propagate in the world, and they are worthy. But we can't move people if we focus on pleasing them. We have to risk their frowns and let them walk away. Until you have made some enemies, you have not done anything significant.'

> Being liked is best as a by-product, not a goal.

I sat down and thought about that for 20 years. I did finally get it. It is, of course, not that we have to be antagonistic, counter-dependent and defiant. That gets no one anywhere. It is rather that we have to have our attention on what we really think and express it hearably and easefully and with compassion, speaking to the goodness in every person. Then we have to listen to them without interruption, with hunger to learn. We have to be ready to tear apart our own views if necessary, reviewing, refining, expressing again, listening again. Then we have to care not a whit about whether or not they like us any more.

> Until you have made some enemies, you have not done anything significant.

That will mean that we make some enemies. Some people hate the people who express the ideas they hate. So we have to be prepared to be hated. Not to look for it. Not to orchestrate it. Just to be fine with it. We need to watch out for the sleeper inclination to distort the expression of our truest thinking in order to be liked. Being liked is best as a by-product, not a goal.

Quakers define friends as people who think for themselves, and say what they think, and listen and learn from and love the goodness in each person. To be a real friend, then, means you have to have enemies. If you don't, you are ironically not being friend enough.

So maybe it is useful to look around now and then and count our enemies – just in case we have postponed our real selves, and thus our glorious journey to meaning.

# Dear Hattie
# Eight

## 'Let It Go'

Be in charge. Let it go.

How do you do both? Aren't they opposites?

No. They are friends. They seek each other. In fact, they cannot live apart. Or in the words of Niels Bohr, 'In shallow truth one thing is true; in deep truth, the opposite is also true.' Meaning lies in paradox.

I think this is how it works. To be in charge is to think through, to be informed. It is to be not in the grip of anything except your own fine mind, your loving heart and all those gorgeous delineated values that are right now tumbling out of your experience and into your plans. Being in charge requires you, yes, to say and be what you believe in most, to ask for and find what you want.

But it also requires you to be able to want what you don't yet know how to want. There are times when what you think you want charges forward so fast it stumbles, falls and rolls like a West Texas tumbleweed, on and on across wheat stubble, no brakes, no brains, no roots, top the same as bottom, halted only because barbed wire held its ground. Trapped, it dries further, dies fully. It is in those times – when what you think you want has taken control of you, and you are desperate – that you need to step back and be open to wanting something else. The hard part of this is that you won't be able to know what that something is. It will come from a place that is you, but bigger than you.

The paradox is that you take charge of your life in those moments by, as Christopher's mother said, 'offering it up'. You hand over the design to that mysterious, but completely dependable, phenomenon that has multiple perspectives, that has more terminals on its desk than you do, that spends at least half of each day roaming and befriending infinity. You stop clutching the by-now frayed Kodak picture you have of the thing, of the relationship, the outcome, the event.

You let it go.

You say to this phenomenon, okay, here it is. Take it. I am happy to receive whatever you conceive that could be even better than this thing I think I want so much. I'll just sit down and lean against this tree here and think about how its roots go down as far as its branches go up and wonder about that while you do whatever it is you do. I'll be here if you need me. (Yes, I know, you won't.)

You trust.

And, you know, if you really, really do trust, if you feel trust and don't just conjure it up as a last resort while still secretly longing for the Kodak thing, if you let go and give power to the greater imagination, creations walk across infinity bridges to you. They take your breath away because clutching control, you could not possibly have thought them up. You did not have enough big information, a frolicking enough view, enough peace, enough expectation.

## Then you stand back and watch. Your job is to marvel.

You were holding on as only fear can make you do. And these possibilities don't come from fear, ever. They come from knowing.

They come from breezes.

I remember when Peter and I needed a building for our Interlocking Curriculum (the group of 32 students that eventually grew into Thornton Friends School). It was already July, and every building we had seen had not worked for some reason. The owner of the last one was still thinking about it. The building was far from ideal, but Peter and I were putting the best spin on it for each other. At least it was a roof and walls, and we could afford the rent with the tuitions we knew we had. And anyway, there was no way, short of a miracle, that the perfect school house was going to show up on our worried doorstep in less than a month.

Then I remembered. I could 'let it go'. It is odd how forgettable that profound concept is. I guess it is such a big step away from victimhood that when you are feeling like a victim it is hard to remember. Anyway, I did that. I sat down right then, right on our front porch looking out at the 100-foot white oaks in our woods and 'worked' until I could feel the way I would feel when the perfect school-house solution came our way. Then I let it go. And got up and walked away, leaving all of that to the universe or whatever the best word is for this thing that outstrips us every time and brings us back to our real power.

And you guessed it. Five days later the phone rang: 'Nancy, this is Bob Johnson. I think I have just what you need. Oak Farm. Have you heard of it? Eighteenth-century big house on a hundred acres. About five miles from you. The only catch is that you will have to make a good impression on the owners. So do you and Peter have college degrees? They seem pretty anxious about that. Not sure why they think college degrees will keep the kids from wrecking the place, but...'

He finally drew breath, and I said yes, felt grateful to Scripps, Amherst and Catholic University; and in 30 minutes Peter and I were walking down the half-mile driveway of the mansion, listening to Bob's stories about Brookeville, and saying thank you in our hearts to that super-view force for the perfect solution. Better than we could possibly have imagined.

I have never made curtains so fast, or stained furniture so fast, or painted walls so fast, or slept so fast. But four weeks later Labor Day arrived, and we were ready, swinging on that antebellum porch, looking at the 322-year-old poplar by the drive and knowing we could easily do the rest – teaching would be no problem.

Letting it go had put us back in charge.

Basically, I guess, the point is that you let go of what you cannot control and trust in whatever that source is that has answers better than yours. And then you stand back and watch. Your job is to marvel.

Christopher and I love the following words commonly (if not entirely accurately) attributed to Goethe, and because they express this concept of trust so well, I want you to have them:

The moment you definitely commit yourself, then Providence moves, too. All sorts of things occur to help you that would never have otherwise occurred. Whatever you can do or dream you can, begin it. Boldness has genius, power and magic in it.

The new paths this offers you are staggering. You do gasp. You do feel your heart somersaulting. But you soon notice that these paths spawned by trust are at once miracles and not miracles at all. They are life, simply. Life in your hands because you can let it go.

I am certain that at the heart of life is this paradox.

To master it is to find meaning you did not know was there.

# Dear Hattie
## Nine

## The F Word

You are a woman. Meaning in your life will come in part from that fact. But what you will want to take into eternity is surely the experience of equality. Deep-down-everywhere-all-of-the-time-no-excuses equality. And until that experience is as embedded as DNA, we will have to approach this meaning of meaning by being smart about it. This means that we have to know our history and see the present for exactly what it is. We cannot be cynical or sentimental. And we have to have fun doing all of this.

So let's begin with this question: Would you describe yourself as a feminist?

I suspect not. Hardly anyone does these days, especially in your generation. Even in mine, the word feminism has become scarce. The concept, accurately defined, on the other hand, has not. The concept shapes my life and yours many times a day. My generation fought for this. Your generation, appropriately, takes it for granted, lives it. Such is the shelf life of collective social change movements. Their relative obscurity is often a sign of their success.

And so I watch your life, and I smile with pride in both our generations. I watch you say what you really think. I hear you describe domestic life and parenthood as an absolutely equal-participation thing. You say that you expect any man to talk honestly with you, to have and share his feelings with you, to negotiate with you rather than control you.

You say that unprotected sex is stupid, and that the safety of your body is not going to be prescribed by anyone but you. You say that in sex 'no' means no, that rape is never caused by women, period. You say that you would leave an abusive or addictive relationship.

You say that you expect to be earning at least as much as your male partner and that manhood has nothing to do with earning. You already have a bank account and credit cards and telephones and a house in your own name.

There is no surprise in your voice when you hear that a woman has become Head of State or Chair of the Board.

You laugh at the women-need-men-in-order-to-be-whole fairy stories, deriding the very idea that a woman could be brought back to life by the kiss of a man. You know that only you can awaken yourself.

You understand the sophisticated analysis that homophobia is actually prejudice against women.

These enlightened attitudes are just who you are. You are not campaigning for them. You don't have to. We did that. And so these things are now your culture. You are living what real feminism can produce. This is wonderful.

But for your generation there is invisible danger. Sexism, the idea that women are inferior to men and must be controlled by men, is not over. It was weakened by our gains, yes; but it lurks. In your generation it has taken to the trees. In your world (though sadly not in many parts of the world where it is still blatant and institutionalized), its war is now mostly a guerrilla war. Its shots come

> Real feminism dignifies both genders.

from places that look safe and lush and inviting.

It lies in language and in pictures. It lies in the eyes of waif-thin, hollow-eyed, tongue-curled cover girls, in the dominance of how-to-get-and-keep-a-male-lover themes of women's magazines. It rests in the definition of a real man as inherently inept at feelings and inherently defaulting to violence.

It inhabits the denigration of women in words like wuss, pussy, sissy, girl, chick, bird because they are used to denigrate men; it is found in the sanctioning of strong-is-best in concepts like winner/loser, weak/strong, we/they, competition-is-needed-for-results-and-collaboration-is-for-sissies assumptions in our global economic systems and in our decisions about war.

It is alive in the still-persistent idea that to help a woman is to do her thinking for her rather than to help her generate her own thinking by listening to her.

It lurks in the words of the invitation to women to join, rather than to change, the ranks of top leadership because the invitation comes with the proviso that women take on the destructive male-conditioned values and structures of corporate culture.

There can be no meaning in life without deep-down equality.

It even skulks, most cunningly of all, inside the phrase 'work-life balance', because that very issue would not exist if women's culture were shaping the structures of economic systems and work places.

It exists in the language of many religions where people are still servants of a male god, where man is subservient to this god and woman is subservient to both, where women are not popes or bishops or mullahs or monks. It is present in the still-taught mythology of women as the source of evil.

And it lies in the repudiation of the word feminist. Just about the time you were born, the definition of feminist was changed from 'a person against the destructive conditioning of both male and female cultures' to 'a woman who hates men'.

And your generation, though benefiting from real (not man-hating) feminism, would not use the word in a million years.

At one level this is too bad. It would be good if the real definition of feminism could emerge. Real feminism dignifies both genders. It is what everyone who wants the best for people wants.

But at another level, it probably doesn't matter. The important thing is that your generation has a new campaign to wage. Your campaign is to expose this insidiousness of silent sexism, to find ways to teach very young children, boys and girls, about the content of gender cultures, the good and the bad, so that they can consider that these ideas have nothing to do with inherent nature, but only with culture, which is changeable.

Your campaign is, most important of all, to bring people together to think differently, to imagine new economic systems that make good lives for all people, to redesign advertising so that it portrays women at their most healthy and powerful, rather than at their most conquered and limp.

Your campaign is to ask the penetrating questions and listen so well that new and never-before-thought-of answers emerge.

My own mother, having fought for women to vote, referred me in the last years of her life to the concept of invisible sexism. 'When I was a girl,' she said, 'women did not have the vote. Fighting for women's suffrage was a huge challenge. But it was easy compared to what you are trying to do. This stage of liberation is the hardest – don't give up.'

There can be no meaning in life without deep-down equality, because there can be no deep-down self-esteem without it. And so, you will want to keep your ears open for the rustlings of invisible sexism.

You will want to say what you hear, and to shake it down, confront it with love, information and confidence. You will want to help create new life systems free of it.

So, I hand to you my mother's encouragement to explore – with your fine mind and strongly held values of respect and love and truth – real feminism, regardless of what we call it. I embrace your generation and mine, both of us holding the same vision of a life of meaning, for everyone.

Such a world, strong and sweet, full of meaning, is possible. I promise.

# Dear Hattie

## Ten

### The Bigger Thrill

'I want to expand. I want to embrace. I am passionate about this work. Whatever it takes, I want to succeed. I want it and me truly to live.' So began Gina's confused relationship with thrilldom. Her words were alive, but her voice was dead. I was curious.

'And the Chair of the Board took me to lunch last week. He said that my work is the finest he has ever seen. He wants to promote it through all seven global learning centres. It is amazing.'

'So why the tentative tone?' I asked.

She looked at me. 'When we said goodbye, he kissed me on the lips. Not long, okay, just slightly lingering, only very slightly. I am sure it was just his version of a kiss on both cheeks. Just an embellishment of thank you for a lovely conversation. Something like that, don't you?'

'I couldn't possibly know,' I said. 'I wasn't there; so the kiss did not bounce off my surveillance nodes. What did yours register?'

'Yeah, well, I don't know.'

'It sounds like you do,' I said.

'Well, maybe, but maybe not; and anyway, I can control what I do about that, whatever it might be, can't I? I can stay in charge of myself, and that is all that matters.'

'How did you feel on your way home? Have you thought just about the work, or some about him, too?' I asked.

'Don't spoil this,' Gina said. 'It is an opportunity of a lifetime to have my work rolled out in this way. He is an intelligent, very experienced executive with the power to make this happen. It was just one stupid, short kiss. I'm sorry I told you.'

I backed off. But I could hear the SOS beneath the ice. Gina was showing every sign of straddling what I like to think of as 'the thrill line'. I want to share that with you. It is a powerful, life-shaping moment each time we find ourselves there.

The moment starts with this sensible-sounding point: 'The opportunity is thrilling. Why shouldn't you go for the thrill when you can?'

Because there is a bigger thrill. It lies on a vertical line. On the right side of the line lie the thrills that will destroy everything on the left side of the line. On the left lies everything you are building and dreaming of and have already accomplished. There, on the left side of the line, lies your reputation, your public, your client base, your strategy, your home, your children, your writing, the letters of appreciation you keep in that special file. Here lies also the perfect balance of passion, prudence, ego, empathy, rootedness and expansion. Here, most important of all, is your trust in yourself.

> Integrity, like discipline, is fired up with life.

Here lie all of the real thrills you would hate most to lose in your life. I say thrills, because those things are thrilling. They get you up in the morning and keep you smiling as you drop off to sleep. They show. They run with you down the hill, your arms and your future wide open. They expand you. And they make your embrace tender.

They do this because they express only you. It is you who is needed there. Only you can build this dream. Not just anyone will do.

The right side of the line, however, hooks its finger and winks. Its lips are sweet. It wants you to step over there. And stay. But it is not you, not the unique you. It needs to be spent and does not care who obliges. Anyone will do.

And right there, just exactly on that line, just before the last bit of right edge, lies the bigger thrill. This thrill thrills when you allow yourself to see its lifelong, life-giving power. It ironically fires up the right side, the lure, because without it this false thrill would not ensnare you.

This bigger thrill is the thrill of integrity. In that moment of decision, that second that takes you from the edge, from 'maybe' to 'no', that optifibre flash of return to yourself, to the left of the line, to your dreams and your influence and the piling of success upon success, to the diamonds in your eyes – to yourself.

So, you can see the invitation; watch its wink; imagine its plot; come near; peer.

Then you can lean back; step just over the vertical line, to the left. You can choose the bigger thrill: treat yourself to that moment when you throw your hat into the air and yelp, when you tap through the puddles and rip open the present. You can choose integrity. You can wake up the next morning with the energy that that bigger thrill engenders. Not with a pounding head and salty heart from agreeing to be just anybody.

When edging to the right, you may feel that this side of the line is big and its offering not to be missed. In fact, its offering is infinitesimal. It is a mirage. And, most important, it cannot expand. It is by nature a shrivelling creature.

Integrity, on the other hand, expands the left side into infinity. Your love of expansion longs for this side of the line. Anything is possible here. All the good things you want are here, some in embryo, developing at unimaginable, invisible speeds.

Integrity, like discipline, is fired up with life. Surely there is no greater thrill, no greater meaning, than that.

# Dear Hattie

## Eleven

### To Be

Given that we all die, how do we find meaning in living? Your beautiful question was essentially about time.

These letters propose that meaning lies beyond time, that it lives in your being you. And so, maybe meaning deepens as we agree not to trap our lives in time, not to measure things too confidently, not to count too often, not to be right too fiercely.

Time does not exist, after all. We make it up. Things do not begin or end. We imagine all of that. Things just are. We just are. And truly to find meaning we have to be willing to be so much in this moment that we shake from its beauty.

When we do experience what we call endings, we need also to be so much with them that we let go of the afterwards. The afterwards we can construct soon enough. It will just be.

You tore time asunder, and just were.

I was walking this morning through the churchyard of a nearly hidden part of Streatley near the River Thames. The second movement of Haydn's Clock Symphony was playing in my head. I suddenly felt Bill with me. Not just by association with death because

115

of the ancient grave stones, and not just because of the little church and its message of eternal life. Nor even because of the transcendent magic of that music. Maybe those were conjurors. But what they summoned was its own self.

It was the ending and the beginning of all things. Our ability to be with and be aware of being with, to think and to think about thinking, to feel and to calibrate feeling, are the quarks of meaning. Our obliviousness to the moment, while noting it, is the entwining that is beginning/ending/beginning.

T S Eliot merged timelessness and meaning this way:

In the end is the beginning
And to make a beginning we make an end

When you were only 14, you knew this. You knew that being with Fred was the way to find meaning in those frightening days and nights. You tore time asunder, and just were.

You can do that always. You can be you.

You can do Hattie exquisitely.

As you do, meaning will find you.

# Kimberley

Today – How Can We Be Happy ?

# Dear Kimberley

## Introduction

You were born one month after I was supposed to die. I didn't die. You were one of the reasons why. Your father, my twin, and your mother, my friend, wanted me to be your godmother. I was honoured. I wanted to live to see you grow up.

You did. And I, gratefully, grew older, each year a private triumph. It has been 42 years and you are exquisite, inside and out, gracing the planet, finding wisdom in your days, reaching for the art, for the soul in each thing, freeing those around you to be themselves – I among them.

*Be happy, happy, happy.*

One day when you were five, you asked me earnestly while we were driving on the edges of the Santa Fe mountains, 'Aunt Nancy, today – how can we be happy?'

With that question you charmed me even beyond your usual five-year-old capacity to make me smile. And you puzzled me. And silenced me. I could see in a flash that to answer you would not be easy. So I faked it. 'Well,' I said, 'we can do what we should do every day,' starting an answer I knew I could not finish.

'What is that?' you asked me back.

'Well,' I said, losing more confidence, 'I guess there are lots of things.'

'Like what?' you persisted.

'Like, well, I can think of several, but they seem kind of philosophical.'

'You mean kind of boring?'

I smiled. 'No, not boring. Not at all. Maybe just grown-up. But we could do lots of other things to be happy today, like pretend to be princesses, or girls with horses, or geologists, or something, couldn't we?'

'Sure,' you said, 'and you can be the horse. Then we can do the boring things later – when I grow up.'

I agreed in a hurry, shelving my thoughts, wanting to get back to them someday, to find my way to real answers to your very real question. Happiness, that one and only goal of human life – how, indeed, can we achieve it today? And tomorrow? And over 40 years, and way beyond?

Happiness has a bad reputation. It is said to be capricious. But I don't think it is. Happiness, I believe, is a decision, an assumption, one we can make at any given second.

What a sweet confluence it was that it was happiness you asked me about, because it was happiness, I believe, that set my path of healing the month you were born. I don't know that I ever told you this, but while I was in the hospital a Chinese doctor arrived in my room, preceded by a full entourage of other Chinese doctors. My own oncological surgeon was away for four days for Thanksgiving, and Peter had slipped in these doctors whose Eastern approaches he thought might help me. The Western world of medicine held out no hope.

Dr Chao examined me in very strange ways, listening for pulses and looking into my eyes and paying no attention whatsoever to my abdomen, which was where the cancer was. I thought he had it wrong. Eventually he stopped and he folded his hands.

He looked at me respectfully and said, 'I can heal you with my herbs. But if you decide not to take that route, please do this.' He paused. He looked at me gently, intensely. He said, 'Be happy, happy, happy.'

He paused again. He smiled. And then he turned to his entourage, rose and left my room.

I felt hope because to be happy, I could see, was within my power. I could decide to do that and, unlike the chemotherapy, offered only experimentally anyway, I knew for sure happiness would not hurt me.

And I guess that is my real answer to your question: happiness is our choice. It is an answer that takes some explicating, deserves lots of stories and requires unbelievable discipline from us. Happiness is an emotion. But it also emerges from rigorous thinking, from relentlessly thinking for ourselves. The rewards are like giants walking the earth. Gorgeous, gentle giants. And, of course, like beautiful horses, too.

I think about your question every day. I find fragments of answers. And I decided that I would piece them together into something coherent, and give them to you so that perhaps they – now that you are over 40, successful in your career, married and a mother yourself – will seem neither abstract nor boring. I hope they will enhance your already-well-expressed set of answers of your own.

They are, most of all, a gift from my heart to yours, paying homage to you now and to the little girl who asked the question.

# Dear Kimberley
## One

### It's Okay

It's weird, but lots of people think it is not okay to be happy. They build their lives on that idea. They go around deciding not to be happy because they are afraid of what will happen to them if they are. Some of my colleagues think that way. Janet said to me one day, 'If I am happy, God will punish me.' She meant it. 'So many people are unhappy,' she said, 'and if I am happy when they are unhappy, I am bad.'

> Happiness is deserved; it is intelligent; it causes only more happiness; it is real.

So, let's see, I thought: a god wants us all to be unhappy until every living other soul is happy? But doesn't that mean that no one will ever be happy because no one can be happy until everyone is, and therefore no one can be first? What kind of a god is that?

Rasa said to me one day, 'I don't deserve to be happy.' I asked her why. She said, 'Because I have not done enough good in the world yet.' I asked her how much good she had left to do. She said, 'I don't know.

But I know I haven't done it yet.'

Really? Don't we deserve to be happy just because we exist? Apparently not. Not according to the law of never-enough.

Then there was Jamie. He said to me, 'Happiness makes you stupid. It consumes you, so you don't notice threats, and then they take you by surprise and you can't think well. So happiness itself is dangerous.' Getting to that conclusion must, I thought, have taken some serious side trips into family culture.

So let's see: happiness is punishable, undeserved and makes you stupid. Wow. Brain science has started to refute this, but I hope it hurries, because Janet, Rasa and Jamie are pretty tense, as you can imagine.

Lisa said something just about as shocking. 'Happiness makes you sad.' Right, I thought. And frowned. 'It goes like this,' she said: 'happiness is always followed by a crisis, always. All you have to do is wait and, sure enough, if you have been feeling happy, something bad will happen. Then the contrast between the pain of the crisis and the joy of the happiness makes the sadness even more acute than it would have been if you had not been happy just before it. So, happiness makes you sad.'

Honestly, I thought. This argument seemed particularly nuts to me because it depends on where you start. Lisa could just as well have started with the crisis and said, 'Every crisis is eventually followed by happiness, always. And the contrast between the joy of the happiness and the pain of the crisis makes the happiness more acute than it would have been if you had not had the pain just before it. So, sadness makes you happy.' I wanted to say to her, 'Remember, *post hoc* does not mean *procter hoc*.' But I didn't.

Then there is the killer argument. Rafi said it: 'Happiness is not real. It is fluff. Only pain is real. And if you indulge in the unreal, you will not be grounded or informed and so you will be unreliable as a thinker about change.' You hear people making this case unawarely all of the time. They say things like, 'Let's get real here.' And they don't mean let's get happy. Or they say, 'I think we are soon going to have to face reality.' And they don't mean we are soon going to have to face how great things are.

So, happiness, according to the lore, is punishable, undeserved, makes you stupid. It is not intelligent; it causes unhappiness; it makes you sad; it is not real. And like lures these lies summon everyone to the shallows. They jump into young minds and persevere until they are grown-up, never able to dry off from the message that happiness is just not okay.

But it is. Very. Happiness is deserved; it is intelligent; it causes only more happiness; it is real.

So let's consider your question with a light heart and clear head. Being happy is definitely okay.

# Dear Kimberley

# Two

## Beginning With Love

This says it. We could just stop here. Love is the text; all the rest is footnote. When we love in this moment, in this day of moments, even if we are not loved back in this moment, we are happy. Love just does that to us. It quells fear. Safe, the brain then sends out hormones like serotonin and oxytocin and endorphins. Love, neurologically speaking, makes us happy.

So what is so hard about deciding to love? What is so alluring about its opposites: fear, rage, resentment, retaliation?

I think it is because, although generating love has helped human beings thrive, generating fear has helped us survive. Surviving precedes thriving.

So I think that part of the brain, the amygdala it is called adorably, has, over these inconceivably long periods of time called human evolution, ended up lacking subtlety. It just does the quickest thing to make sure we don't get killed: it interprets undangerous things as dangerous. Someone criticizes you and your brain assumes they may kill you. It sends out hormones to

Love is the text; all the rest is footnote.

make you get out or strike out. (Those are the unhappy hormones like adrenaline and cortisol.) And those hormones shut down your reasoning, so you can't get how undangerous that moment actually is. You can no longer see the safety all around you, the reality of your being a wholly good and wonderful person still, and your being loved beyond all measure. You cannot think for yourself.

In that moment happiness leaves you because you cannot feel love. You cannot give love either. Nor can you take it in. In that moment love drains from the whole world.

Nature was accidentally clever in a way, to make the brain so trigger-happy in its interpretation of danger. It has meant that we got this far as a human species; we were not wiped out by the real dangers. We got out or struck out.

But the whole thing now lacks nuance. And we have to override the survival trigger and provide that nuance. Fortunately, we are well equipped to do that. Along with the trigger comes the finely tuned, stunningly sophisticated ability to notice our fear and assess the situation with a different part of our brain, the cortex.

With this amazing cortex we can decide to do three things:

We can look right at the danger and see it for the nothing that it is. We can get interested in it as a kind of pathetic phenomenon. Gosh, we can think, how amazing: Sally is criticizing me; she is angry; she is blaming me for all those things. Isn't that interesting? I wonder what she is assuming that is causing her to act like that toward me. I wonder what she will say next. I wonder what I can learn from this about myself.

We can go back to noticing our own fear and look at it from every angle: wow, we can say, this is amazing; I have stopped loving this person and I am feeling scared of her as if she could end my life. I wonder what I am assuming that is causing me to feel afraid? Oh, I am assuming that I don't matter any more, that I am now of no value, that I am not smart or lovable or anything anyone would want. Is all of that true, we can wonder? Of course not, we can realize.

So what is true instead? I exist and matter as much as I did just a few minutes ago. I am 100 per cent fine. If I knew that I am 100 per cent fine, how would I feel listening to Sally? If I knew that I am 100 per cent fine, how would I act in this moment? What would I say when she is finished? And we will know. We just will. And if we act on that knowing, our brains will begin, if gradually, to replace the unhappy hormones with the happy ones and the fear will subside.

So, the third option: we can then decide to notice all of the things we love about Sally. And we can focus on those, hardly noticing the temporary monster that is in our path at the moment. We can focus on what we love until we can feel again that we love her. And the love will make us happy.

All prophets think that love is the key to happiness and sanity. Jesus, the prophet I know about, went all the way with that idea. He said we should love Sally no matter what. 'Love your enemies,' he said, 'and pray for those who persecute you.' Think about that. Really think about it. That, and the other things he said about love, would take us centuries to learn and more centuries to live. In fact it has: 20 centuries and counting. (And some days aren't you appalled at the brazenly unloving things many people called Christians do to people?) Love your enemies. Amazing thought. Which ones exactly did he mean, do you suppose?

Well, for sure he meant Sally. She would be the starting place. Loving her when she is savaging us would be a good workout for the really tricky enemies, like all those foreigners who might drop bombs on us (or would those foreigners be us?). And to do this we have to notice what we do love about each other, regardless of the craziness of one of us at the moment. Jesus was smart. Very. I'll bet he would have been fascinated to learn that love produces the hormones that get the brain thinking and feeling intelligently.

When we love our enemies, we get to be happy. And when we are happy, we love our enemies. It is a sweetly disturbing, life-giving cycle.

So, if we want to be happy today, I think we can choose to begin each day with love. We can remember as the day begins that the thinking we do as we wake can produce the assumptions that produce the hormones that produce the happiness.

So tomorrow when you wake up, you can grab your thoughts and focus them on what you love. You can focus on the people you love, of course. And on the people you have a hard time loving, and love them just a tiny bit more than you did yesterday. And you can focus also on the little things you love – the silk, the skin on your arms, the sky. And then feel the happiness that starts to hum.

You can begin with love.

Then you can choose.

# Dear Kimberley

## Three

## What You Really Need

You matter as much as anyone else. Take that in. Let it lean you in one direction: toward a fathoming of what you really need. Every day. Really every day. Start with the question:

If I knew that my needs are as important as anyone else's, how would I spend my day?

Maybe you do this already. But you would be the exception, even in your generation. For all the advances women have made since your birth (and they are to be celebrated and not taken for granted for a second), messages call out to us from every

Asking and then listening to your own answers is an advanced skill of womanhood.

medium, in ever more subtle and insidious ways, telling women to sacrifice themselves and their needs and dreams, and sometimes their sanity, for the key men and children in their lives, and in some cases for the highest paid and most prestigious position they can achieve.

And so, even for your generation, deciding what you truly need, and whose needs to put first in a given moment, is a tricky thing.

This is ironic, because when we don't know that our needs matter as much as anyone else's, and we just keep meeting theirs, we can lose energy; we then serve those very people poorly. This is probably because in assuming our needs are not as important as the needs of others, we betray ourselves. And when we betray ourselves, we almost instantaneously blame the others we are prioritizing as if they were the reason we betrayed ourselves in the first place.

When we betray ourselves, we betray ourselves. Period. No one makes us do it. And no one but us can undo it. The pre-flight oxygen-mask thing is boring, but it is no joke. We cannot meet others' needs unless we can breathe.

Sometimes even figuring out what we really need is no joke, either. But the question at the beginning of this chapter is a big help, hour to hour even. It is the question that shaped your decision to be a model. It is the question that shaped my regime to survive. So, I recommend it. You can start every day with it, or end every day with it as you think about tomorrow. You can ask your mind and heart to speak, and then listen to them. Your answers will be perfect for you. But only if they are your answers, not if they are answers to please others or not frighten or confuse them. Asking and then listening to your own answers is an advanced skill of womanhood.

> You matter as much as anyone else.

Call Aunt Merl if you want some encouragement. Yesterday her answer to the question was, 'Open a new bank account and keep a $200 balance in it no matter what.' That was the important part: 'no matter what'. She was pretty irrepressible by the time she got home from the bank. The energy came from asking the question and listening to the answer, and then doing it. It was a lifting of censorship – of herself.

Self-betrayal sucks energy right out of us. Self-honouring restores and increases it. It is that simple.

And it is one far-reaching way to be happy today.

# Dear Kimberley
## Four

### The Dig

Getting beneath hard stuff is hard. And there is probably something, maybe even something big, you struggle with but can't see under. That is the stuff that can do-in happiness. It sits there like a crumbly monolith, pointing to nothing. It growls, in a Marge Simpson sort of way. And we kind of hear it. But we can take ages walking around it. Or pretending that it isn't important. Or that we can live with it, even though it blocks lots of views, bulbous monstrosity that it is.

> We have to decide to wonder about what we can't see.

So we have to get ruthless. We have to decide to look straight at this thing, and wonder what holds it in place, because it is not the thing itself that is the problem. It would fall over if it weren't anchored. So we have to decide to wonder about what we can't see. That is usually stuff about ourselves. We have to dig.

This digging is different from the Amy Question kind. This digging necessitates a particular desire, a courageous desire to know what we don't yet know. It is this desire that softens the ground, sharpens the shovel and brings us strawberries to keep us going. We have to want to know what is real. We have to want that more than we are scared of being wrong. Most important of all, we have to know that we can handle what we find.

One of the hardest things I ever had to face was when I was in an addictive organization. (Learning about those, by the way, is a good idea in itself. Making sure you don't join or become one is also good – and goes a long way toward being happy today, I can tell you.) I thought it was committed to increasing the mental health and general wellbeing of people. I had for several years let the leader's presentation of the situation be my view.

Then one day I faced it: he was having an illicit relationship with scores of female members of the organization and had created an inner circle of these accomplished women who agreed to secrecy about this. There. Giant monolith faced. Next job: dig to see what is keeping it in place. Discovery: the assumption that leaders and experts are smarter than I am, and that my perceptions are naïve, unsophisticated and dismissible. Next job: get rid of those assumptions. Next job: get out of the organization. Next job: look for the next monolith; see it as a monolith. Dig it out. Next job ....

We have to decide to look and to see, to dig and then to say three words to ourselves: this is so.

The challenge is that this process is subtle. Information is always loaded. It comes dressed in expertism, in final-wordism, in you'd-better-because-I-say-so-and-I-know-more-than-you-doism, in higher-degreeism. When it does, it is dangerous. Information, to be useful, has to be inclusive of its implications and clean in its context. Raw data is no help. It looks smart, but standing alone it is stupid. The implications of the data have to be full, accurately drawn and understood. Also, the people drawing the conclusions need to have no, and I mean no, investment in those conclusions – not reputation, not job security, not profit, not feelings, not fixes.

An expert's view is just a view. It can inform, but not dictate, our own. So if you are told by the expert or the leader that something is appropriate, but that it would be misunderstood by the uninitiated and so needs to be secret, you can do your own thinking about this: you can decide only to factor in what the expert says, not to swallow it whole and ignore the nausea. You, Kimberley, may think that as a model and a mother you are unlikely to encounter this addictive-leadership phenomenon. But leaders and experts of all kinds, addicted to one thing or another – power, work, control, fame, alcohol, sex – are more common than you, or anyone else, might think.

There also are other versions of the digging challenge. If you notice something about your body, for example, that doesn't seem right, you can start from that minute to think for yourself. You can find out what you want to know from the widest possible range of 'experts', including your inner knowledge and wisdom. Then you can lay all the opinions and analysis and conclusions on your table, ask ruthless questions about their context and about the author's investment in the conclusion. You can watch some of the answers destroy the conclusion, and some of them support it. You can determine which is a monolith. Then you can dig. And you can insist that everyone else step back while you look below the toppled thing yourself.

Our own view, arrived at through the dismantling and conceiving of a multiplicity of things, some objective, some ineffable, requires the deepest digging. Monoliths collapse in the face of our total understanding. Then we get to clear away the rubble, fill in the hole, plant a tree and dance off, happy today, maybe all week – maybe all of our lives.

# Dear Kimberley

## Five

## 'Get Up Off The Sofa'

My colleague Scott Farnsworth, a genius at getting lawyers to listen, has taught me so many important things, I probably should just figure out a way to wrap him up in this book and send him to you. All of those things, no matter where he discovered them, have profound implications for work and love and study and play, everything. This particular gem came from Sunday lunch. He offered it to me because I was stumped by how dependably people in long relationships get into the same sour conversation loop with each other over and over again, for a lifetime.

He told me that he had figured out what to do about that. 'Marcie and I used to have lunch with her family every Sunday,' he said. 'And after lunch we moved from the dining room into the living room to talk. And every time, as soon as we all got settled in and had said how good the lunch was, we got onto some subject, it didn't matter what it

> As soon as I recognize the same old linear road to nonlinear places, I move.

was, that seemed to uncap a cavernous, complaining, crankiness well in us. And down we all went, until we crashed at the bottom in a heap of rancour. Every time. No matter what I tried to do to change the subject or lighten the tone, we all fell in.

'Then one day I noticed that not only was the conversation the same, but so was where each of us was sitting in the living room. Same sofa place, same chairs. So Marcie and I agreed that the next Sunday I would get up off the sofa and we would sit in different chairs.

'We did it. As soon as the conversation began, we moved. And it was as if the cranky conversation couldn't quite get going. It kept falling all over itself somehow. It could not get its bearings. And when we then focused the topic differently or changed the subject or got funny, the conversation rolled over like a Lab, compliant as anything.

'So,' he said, 'I think that when we are stuck in dull, or even destructive, behaviour in our relationships, we can decide just to "get up off the sofa."'

He is right. I have done this now many times, always with amazing results. As soon as I hear that familiar tone of voice in myself or the other person, as soon as I recognize the same old linear road to nonlinear places, as soon as I feel that creepy combination of boring and frustrated, I move. Physically. I may just stand up. I may walk across the room, I may get on the floor, but I move.

And like magic, the tone, the words, the pauses, the listening, something, changes immediately, and the conversation moves differently. It is as if we become conscious of our footing. I am sure it has something to do with creating new perspective, taking a breath, letting go. The controls change. We have to wake up and see the new dashboard. It's something. I don't quite know.

But it can bounce us right off sad and into happy, that I am sure of.

# Dear Kimberley
## Six

## Every Wrinkle

You are 42 years old now. You are beautiful. You are a model. And I am wondering how you are feeling about the wrinkles that are moving, silently, like tiny tributaries into your face. I am wondering whether you know that your face is more beautiful than ever.

I wonder whether you have decided to love every wrinkle, to see each one as a sign of increased beauty. I wonder whether you actually love each one. I wonder if you love nature's changes. And I wonder what it would take for the whole world to love them, too.

> We need old women to show us how to be beautiful.

I tried out that idea at *Cosmopolitan* once. I had been hired to spend three hours with the magazine's editorial staff, including the Editor-in-Chief. They wanted me to teach them how to have conversations in a Thinking Environment so that everyone could think independently on issues important to women.

Trusting that they meant it, I arrived, taught them about Generative Attention and Incisive Questions. That took about an hour. Then

I sent them off to the corners of the room to think, with a question and a partner. One was to be the listener, asking the question, staying interested, never interrupting; one would be the thinker, going to the edge of her own thinking. The question was:

If you and the world knew that you are beautiful exactly as you are, what would change for you?

There was a lively buzz. Then they switched roles, more ideas from the new thinker, more generative Attention from the new listener.

When the time was up and they were back in the circle of chairs, each of them shared, in a round with no interruption or cross-talk, their freshest answer to the question. The answers were dazzling. 'I would walk with more grace; I would think about something other than what other people think of my looks; I would decide what I really want to do with my life and do it immediately; I would figure out what to do with all of that time, the time I spend worrying about my looks and buying things to fix them; I would cry with relief; I would never again judge another woman.'

## Wrinkles are beautiful. Who, with any credibility at all, says they aren't?

Then the Editor-in-Chief spoke. 'If I and the world knew that I am beautiful exactly the way I am...' She paused. She looked around the group of her editors. She continued, '...we would go out of business.'

No one laughed. No one moved. I smiled as if an asteroid had not just hit the planet. I went to the next person in the round. She passed. I went to the next. She passed. All three remaining people passed.

I proposed discussion about the topic. No one spoke.

So I did a speedy little wrap-up lecture, wished them well and got out of there. Safely in the taxi, I breathed. I decided not to cry, although I was pretty sure taxi drivers had seen worse. Instead I did a quick debrief with myself. Maybe, I thought, that was not exactly the best question for a lunch-time workshop. Actually, maybe that was not exactly the best question for *Cosmopolitan* at any time of any day. You think? I felt embarrassed. Then I felt pleased.

Beauty. I pondered it. It is a human construct. I don't care what people say about newborns responding to certain facial features more than to others, human beings make up what beauty is, and sell it. We sell it first culturally, in our relationships and schools and parties and religions. We sell it literally, through products and their advertisements in the *Cosmos* of this world. We make money from the deep looks-inadequacy we instil in every female on earth. Of every age.

And especially females over 30. The market is massive and on its knees. Women over 30, especially over 40 and desperately over 50, will do just about anything to look the way the magazines say to look. And as I could see from the answers the editors shared that day, women's lives are enslaved by this Sisyphean heave of being beautiful in arbitrary eyes.

Strangely, it doesn't matter how close to the constructed standard of beauty a woman gets; she still feels less-than. And the older she gets the more less-than she feels. That is why I wonder how you are feeling as you settle into your forties. I know women who stop having birthday celebrations after 40. I know hundreds who dread each year. All of them are effectively hating nature. Nature intended us to wrinkle and blotch and shorten. And with just the slightest switch in society's definition, those changes would be celebrated, not desecrated. Even the most experimental adopting of the view that to live to be old is to live to be beautiful – truly, physically, enviably beautiful – would liberate whole lives.

Maybe we all just need to come close, very, very close to dying when we are young. Wrinkles are the best thing in the world then. They shout, they leap, they drum the good news that we are alive! And that makes it easy to see that they are beautiful. Maybe that is why I love them.

My friend Margaret Legum taught me to love them, too. She did this just by living. I visited her in South Africa when she was in her seventies. We went to the beach. She took off her shirt and skirt and ran out into the sea in her bathing suit, her arms waving to me to join her. I just stood there, transfixed – not because the water is from the Antarctic and seizes up every pulmonary impulse God gave you. I stood transfixed by her walking and running and just being in all those wrinkles. Every part of her body, except her eyeballs, undulated. Crepe everywhere.

Could I, I wondered, for all my philosophical positioning on the subject of age, ever feel that pleased about my body when it began to look like that? And, if I could, could I go the next step and expect the rest of the world to love every wrinkle too? Or could I, even better, not care what anyone thought, but just saunter and run and live in my exposed body according to the truth, knowing that one day, long after I am dead probably but it doesn't matter, everyone will know that freedom? The freedom that only truth can produce?

Then about six years later, I noticed (and it must have been going on a long time, but I had not looked down with my eyes wide open) that my thighs were seriously wrinkled. And my first thought was not, 'Oh, no!'

My first thought was, 'How cool, I look like Margaret!'

We need old women to show us how to be old. We do not need old women to show us how to be young. We need old women, most importantly, to show us how to be beautiful.

So, I wonder if each morning you wake, go to the mirror, search for new wrinkles and, if you find one, do a teensy hooray, just between you and nature, to celebrate. Why? For one thing, because it is true: wrinkles are beautiful. Who, with any credibility at all, says they aren't?

For another, being happy today depends on it. For all of the women in that *Cosmopolitan* circle, and all women of every age everywhere, moments of happiness, days and nights and years of happiness, depend on letting the beauty-is boulder fall, and refusing to push it back up the mountain.

Being happy today depends, in fact, on walking away from the mountain itself, and considering that Incisive Question, even before breakfast:

If you knew that you are beautiful just as you are, how would you live today?

# Dear Kimberley
## Seven

### 'Expect Nothing'

Christopher taught me this: to be happy we have to stop having expectations of others, especially our parents. They are never going to get it right for us and, once we face that, we can be happy. And then, when the expecting-nothing frame is fully functional, we can notice that they actually do get it right – occasionally. But that is a bonus. Bonuses are very different from salary.

At his wholehearted suggestion his ageing parents had moved into half of his house. He weekended in his half, living and working in London during the week. For two years he noticed that on the road to work each Monday morning, he was furious with his parents. He could not trace the fury to anything.

Then one Monday he heard himself thinking, 'Why can't they just occasionally do the simple things that make a big difference to me? Is it so bad to expect a minuscule amount of awareness from them?'

Then he saw moving gently across his mind two words that would change his life: 'Expect nothing.'

From that moment, he did just that. Whoever they were was whoever they were; whatever they noticed was whatever they noticed; however they responded was just that. That was all. They weren't being thoughtless; they were just being. And sure enough, as soon as he stopped expecting anything of them, he noticed how thoughtful of him they were in other ways. He had missed those when the longing/resentment cycle had consumed the view. And he was happy, especially on the road on Monday mornings. In one single lifting of the scrim, he had changed the scene. Expecting nothing had produced everything.

This is a fascinating feature of being happy. It is, I think, a version of letting go, of facing the sobering but liberating fact that we cannot, we should not and we'd better not try to construct other people. Instead we can, we should and we'd better just be present, notice what is, ponder it, respond lovingly and astutely to it, and get on with constructing ourselves. Our happiness gets mired and wired and tired when it is jerked around by our need for other people to be, act, think or feel in an ordered-by-us way. They just won't. And that is that.

> Expecting nothing had produced everything.

So if we don't like the way other people are, we can just change the way we relate to them, including exiting if we need to. Happiness gets chewed up mostly by disappointment. And disappointment is an entirely self-inflicted injury. No one can disappoint us. Only our fabricated versions of people can disappoint us. We try to create other people and they refuse to be created because they already exist. That is all disappointment is. And it is wholly avoidable. We just need to stop playing God and Mother Nature and let God and Mother Nature do the work they already have done.

Like the universe, everything comes from nothing. It is really simple.

# Dear Kimberley
## Eight

### I'll Get Back To You

In the 1980s a woman in San Francisco made an important discovery. A biochemist, Lydia Temoshok, was researching the lives of people with HIV. She found that when people say yes when they want to say no, their immune systems weaken. Doing unwanted favours, as she called the behaviour, actually jeopardizes the work of T-helper cells, killer cells and lymphocytes.

Over 25 years, she and other researchers have concluded that passivity, victimization and resignation – the practice of pleasing others and displeasing ourselves – can cause and advance cancer (most likely an immune-deficiency disease). Conversely, people who decide to stay happy by not agreeing to do what they deeply do not want to do, have more active, healthy immune responses to lethal viruses. How exciting is that?

It seems Dr Chao (the Chinese herbalist) was right. Your immune system insists that you be happy. If you aren't, it loses bits of itself.

So – no martyrs allowed. And this is no easy thing. Deciding not to do what others want us to do that we do not want to do gets all tied up with teachings about selfishness. But this is more sophisticated, more subtle, than selfishness. This is a matter of caring for ourselves, not caring *only* for ourselves. It is an act of conversation between our deepest needs and the demands of others. It is an act of self-respect, and self-respect is complex. So we have to think about it.

We have to think well and fast, because doing what others want us to do is often a bullet-quick decision. Someone asks a favour, or proposes an activity, or offers a relationship, and fearing that a pause in our response will devastate them, and needing to please everyone in the whole world in order to believe we are good enough, we hear ourselves saying, 'Sure' before the print-out from our heart has even figured out all the digits.

> Your immune system insists that you be happy.

But with practice we can learn to handle these moments with the subtlety they contain. We can even be lithe, eventually. I am still practising. I have moved forward considerably from my earlier not-so-lithe approach. One afternoon I arrived at my dressmaker's house. She was an ace dressmaker. And her husband was an ace cook. The three of us sometimes talked about his and Christopher's cooking. It was all very nice.

Then on this day, as I walked through the living room balancing a pile of slacks to be shortened, Sam walked out of the kitchen, greeted me warmly and said, 'Nancy, Joan and I would like to invite you and Christopher to dinner one evening. Would you like to tell us when you might have an evening free in the next couple of months?'

I froze. I stood there as if someone had just said they were going to build a freeway through our garden. And I could not figure out in that first second what was happening to me. Then it hit me – this is one of those Temoshok moments.

I could see it all unfolding: I knew that I would go home and tell Christopher about the invitation and we would talk about it; then we would try to find a date that would be sooner than the return of Christ; then we would decide listlessly to give up one of the precious evenings that punctuate our monstrously busy work lives, evenings we barely are able to find for our closest circle of friends and family; then we would say yes and feel angry at Sam and Joan for inviting us; then we would go to dinner; then feel that we had to find another evening to have them in return; then know that this had set up an expectation that we would do all of this again; and the pretence would plough on. Eventually, we would stop answering the phone for fear it would be another invitation for dinner with them.

I stood there inert, smiling, in order not to hint for a second that I had just zoomed through a war zone. Then amazingly I decided to do the greatest act of disaster prevention since Dr Robin Spence's creation of earthquake-resistant architecture. I said, 'Thank you so much, Sam; but you know, that is just never going to happen.'

His face went from elated to deflated in a way that almost made me recant. I wanted to rescue him so much that I nearly dropped all of the slacks and said yes. I did say that we never have free evenings any more, and I am glad I added that. But even so, his face lifted only a smidgeon and I feared I might never again walk into that house and be greeted by his usual wide, wonderful smile.

But I also knew that was a small price to pay for being true to what was true. I had not done an 'unwanted favour'. Whew. It seemed to me I could almost feel the T-helper cells and lymphocytes mopping up the adrenaline and rejoicing not to have been decimated by a wishful-thinking 'yes.'

My approach, though, clearly needed work.

And over time I realized that it is even more true to self to give ourselves time. It is fine just to say, 'Thank you so much. I will get back to you about that.' Even when we already know that we don't want to do whatever it is, we have the right to ease the moment by saying, 'I'll think about it.'

Then we can go home and think about how we want to say no. In that way we can handle the whole thing without even a single T-cell biting the dust.

And then we can start over being happy today.

# Dear Kimberley
## Nine

### 'Have What You Have'

Happiness, according to three giants in philosophy, is a state of not wanting more than you have. Epicurus, Zeno and Epictetus all said so.

'That which is happy must possess in full all that it wants,' Epictetus said. 'He must resemble a person who has achieved his fill.'

Darrin McMahon, paraphrasing these giants, said, 'By radically restricting the number of our total wants, we help ensure our ability to satisfy them in full.'

This is fascinating to me. Does it say that we should not aspire, not dream, not set our sights high? Does it say that we should shave our own sense of what we can be, of how we can experience life? To be happy, if we believe Epictetus, is to have no longing, no yearning for what we do not have. We fail to be happy when we focus on what we don't have. Happiness, he seems to think, lies in having fully what we have.

But if we don't long for what we don't have, wouldn't things-society collapse? Isn't the point of things-society to make us compare ourselves to each other and then to strive to keep up or to stay in the lead? Aren't we supposed to feel bad about what we do have so that we can be made to want what we don't have? Isn't it advertising's job to get us to want what we hadn't even thought of wanting, to see that others have it and to lure us to find a way, healthy or not, to get it?

Then don't we have to make the people without the more feel they are less? These are the putrescent tentacles of competition – flailing, looking for flares, lost. And we are so inside its reach we do not see its suckers.

So, let's revisit Epictetus. Does happiness really require us not to long for what we do not have? And what does it mean to have fully what we do have? Does happiness preclude our ever buying another new thing again?

No. It means only that we refuse to be made to long for, to covet. It means refusing to equate having the thing we do not have with having ourselves. It means stopping, taking in, being with, touching, talking to each thing we do have. It means recognizing that we need nothing more because we have all we need. And we do.

When I say we, of course, I mean you and me and the rest of this tiny part of the human population that does have all it needs. Epictetus was speaking to that tiny population, too, even in the first century,

> It means refusing to equate having the thing we do not have with having ourselves.

because it is that part, our part, that continues, now more fiercely than ever, to put its intelligence and creativity and energy into making our tiny part want more, instead of figuring out how, truly and in resplendent, never-before-thought-of ways, all of humanity can have all it needs; and then all of us can reach sensibly for more without depriving others as we reach.

So, I think we can start this particular road to being happy by being with all we have. And if we find, after communion with that thing, that we do not want it any more, we can be sure it gets to someone who does.

And then we can sit down and think, really think, about the things we want that we don't have. We can refuse to want them if we can tell that we have been made to want them.

## Having what we have is an art.

We can refuse to want them if it is actually love we are longing for, or meaning, or permission to say who we are, or silence, or sky, or time, or even a fresh slice of ginger.

Having what we have is an art.

Happiness is, too. They live in each other, I think.

# Dear Kimberley

## Ten

## Being With The People You Are With

It used to be, not so long ago (about a year), that having lunch with my friend meant having lunch with my friend. It did not mean having lunch with 30 other of her friends, none of them invited. Nor did it mean having lunch with 3,000 also uninvited strangers. We had invited only each other. We arrived, we hugged hello, we talked, laughed, listened to each other beautifully, generated coherent threads of conversation, allowed some of it to go deeply, reflected, laughed some more, enjoyed the occasional silent moments, hugged goodbye and left. And our friendship grew, lunch by lunch. That's how it used to be.

No more. These days I never know who else will turn up, or how long they will stay. These days her attention is choppy; our conversation doesn't deepen; our thoughts don't completely cohere. She is engaging with all these other people.

The last time we met, I realized that this influx of people into our lunches was also making me feel unimportant, sidelined, dismissible. I could no longer trust her attention, and so I began not quite to trust her. Then I began to feel angry. Our friendship was shrivelling, lunch by lunch.

So the last time we met, the moment I saw her put her smartphone on the table, I said, 'I don't want to be with you unless it is you I am with. Only you. Just for these 90 minutes.' I was shaking. It seemed a bold thing to do. Ridiculous. Bold to insist that if we are with each other, it is each other we are with. Bold to insist that our attention be continuous for each other so that we can go places in our thinking, in our conversation, that fragmentation and interruption prevent. Bold to ask for friendship. Bold to stand up to the 'smart' phone.

I know we all love our digital lives. I love mine, too. But they can be like lanceheads in the Amazon: in our night they can fall into our hammocks and kill us.

Linda Stone would agree. Researching the effects of the importunities of always-on messaging she has called this mode of being 'continuous partial attention' or CPA. She is worried. She is noticing what we all are noticing, but she is saying it out loud. She is worried because people are all of the time in a state of partial attention for everything. She finds that people are less and less able to give each other full attention. This worries her because she knows that humans cannot develop thought unless we can focus and unless we are given continuous full attention as we think.

## We need to decide to be with the people we are with.

It seems, too, that this is now at the level of addiction. She finds that we are addicted to 'not missing anything'. The actual chemical addiction is to the adrenaline that this fear of missing something triggers in our brains.

The irony is that by responding to every bleep and ping in order not to miss things, we are missing the most important things of all: the ideas and insights, creative gems and profound connections that cannot breathe themselves into life in the jolts of interruption.

I go even further. I worry because adrenaline rushes do not lead to happiness. We think they will. They seem to for a while. But soon they exhaust us, and they betray us. They make us think that things are exciting when they aren't. They strip us of our capacity to discern meaning or to generate depth. They make us fear silence and ease, both of which are where brilliance is born.

Lunchtime with a friend is one thing. Evening time with family is frighteningly another. I visited another friend recently. She was on the sofa. In one hand was her Blackberry; in the other was the TV remote control; on the coffee table in front of her was her laptop; and sitting next to her was her son saying, 'Mother, Mother, listen to me.' 'Just a minute,' my friend snapped.

She continued to read a tweet, replied and flipped the TV channel to the stock report. 'Okay,' she said, 'what is it?' Her son took a breath, tried to find his words, said 'um' a lot and then her smartphone pinged and my friend looked at the message. Her son got up and went back to his room. My friend stayed on the sofa, inputting and calling to her son to come back. I went to bed.

> Adrenaline rushes makes us fear silence and ease, both of which are where brilliance is born.

Being a parent, giving attention adequately to each child, is hard no matter what. Demands on parents' attention are never meet-able. But add digital messaging and CPA to the mix, and we have a surreal and unprecedented platform of family disconnection. We have truncation of fine thought. We have the makings of unhappiness that are falling unnamed and invisible into our hammocks. If we don't wake up and move, they will kill our relationships.

If happiness – real happiness – is our goal, we need to decide to be with the people we are with, to honour them and ourselves by continuous full attention and its fruits. We need to press the off button and slip the wondrous tyrannical things into our pockets. The uninvited guests will still be there for us to engage when it is legitimately their turn.

# Dear Kimberley
## Eleven

### Success

People are forever trying to decide for us what success is. And they are always wrong. We are the only ones who will ever know when we are successful. We are the only ones who can even define the word for ourselves. There is no, I repeat, no, externally determined correct definition of success. To determine it for ourselves takes an astonishing amount of independent thinking. And that takes an even more astonishing amount of silence from others while we think.

It is my impression that you did think for yourself about success. You chose to be a model; you chose your husband thoughtfully; you chose to have children. And by any measure you are already successful. From your symphonically loving soul to your magic with physical space; from your global reach as a model to your second-by-second mothering, you are worthy of emulation.

> There is no, I repeat, no, externally determined correct definition of success.

And now? What do you still want to do or to be? What might success look like for you over the next 20 years? And just as importantly, how will you define your children's success?

It is often as mothers that women claim no longer to have choice about what they do and where they succeed; and just as often they feel they cannot claim success as a mother either.

So it is worth returning consciously and often to the only arbiter of your success there is: you. It is not easy. The older we get, and the more that is expected of us in the doing-for-others department, the more jealously we have to squeeze tight the right to think for ourselves relentlessly about it. This question helps:

If I knew that only I can define it, what would success be for me?

And then we have to dismiss, ignore, rebuff anyone else's ideas about it. Also relentlessly.

What do you have when you stand alone and figure it out for yourself? How true can you be to your right to your own thinking?

Enough questions. Time for thinking. Time for silence.

# Dear Kimberley
## Twelve

### Three Words

Christopher's twin brother, Peter, stood to make the speech at their niece's wedding reception. After ten minutes of extremely funny (and affectionate) stories about Emma, Peter became very serious, almost romantic, and ended with this:

'Now as you go from this day forward into the joys and challenges of married life, you will find that every day your happiness will deepen if you can just remember to say, more often than you may ever feel comfortable saying, three little words. Many people are reluctant to say them. But these three words can lift a heart, heal a wound, restore peace, and restart kind conversation....'

As I listened to him, I found myself melting, feeling how important it is to me that C and I say, 'I love you' many times a day, every day.

A consummate comedian, Peter was surprising me with this switch to sentiment.

He continued, 'And these three little words are...,' he paused.

I squeezed Christopher's hand.

'You're...probably...right,' Peter said.

Of course the place erupted. I thought of how you would have loved it, too. It was funny not just because we didn't see it coming, but because it is true – and hard: these words are usually not said, and they are powerful. 'I love you' is powerful, too, of course, and too rare; but these other three little words are a different challenge altogether.

## Conceding is not surrender. It is acknowledgement.

What it takes to say them (and it works best if it is not just one of you in the relationship that says them; giving and receiving is what creates the happiness) is wide-angled perspective. It is placement in the future. It is self-confidence and ease, a desire to keep communicating rather than to win. What it takes to say, 'You're probably right' is nothing less than grace.

And it is not just the words. Tone matters, too. It would not, for example, be what Bah and her siblings said to each other in arguments. Bah told me that when she was fed up with contentious points of view from Aunt Corabell or Uncle Murray, she would put her hands on her hips and kind of sway from side to side, saying in a sing-songy sort of way: 'You're right; you're always right; you know, because you know everything.'

That wouldn't do it, really, not if happy is how you both want to feel at the end of it. 'You're probably right' has to drain itself of self-righteousness in order to make the Peter Spence magic.

'You're probably right' works because it really isn't magic. It is truth, a truth that is intended for a particular moment of disagreement. It is the moment when you face the wobbliness in your own thinking and the strands of soundness in theirs. The wobbliness is fear, a typical misreading, stupid and out of all proportion to reality: we are not dying here, or even disappearing.

We are just conceding a point in a forgettable argument with a person we love a lot, maybe more than anyone else in the world. What is real, what is true, is that if we concede what is accurately concede-able, we push up new terrain on which to explore the subject afresh, and then build something, something unlike anything we could have sketched out before we conceded.

Conceding is not surrender. It is acknowledgement. It allows us to breathe so that we can be more intelligent.

And happy.

# Dear Kimberley
## Thirteen

### Movement

My friend Julie had a baby girl and then a baby boy. She and her husband had very little money. Nevertheless, they saved some each month. I assumed it was for the babies' health care, or for their college education (your grandfather, before he and Bah had us, had insisted there be no conception, even, until they had saved enough money for the yet-to-be-conceived child to go to college – did you know that?), or at least for Christmas.

But when I asked her, she said, 'We are saving for the children's therapy.' She went right on putting away the dish in her hand as if everyone in the world did this.

'Their therapy?' I asked, trying to sound intrigued rather than incredulous.

'Yes,' she said, 'think about it. Parents inevitably mess up their children. And they are trying like mad not to. They are forever trying to hold things together and line things up just right. But life's too short and too exhausting and too confusing and too full of possibility to try to get everything right. Anyway, it isn't possible. What is right for one child is not always right for the other. And the range of needs among the four of us is epic.

'So we decided that instead of trying to make hospital corners out of our children's lives while denying the inevitable messes we are making, or warping all of us with risk aversion, we would just face the fact that we are doing unwitting damage, but that therapy can usually rectify early childhood stuff well enough to shake out a reasonably happy adult. And since the damage is not the child's fault at all, we figure we should finance the rectification.' One more dish into the cabinet. Then a smile.

'Get it now?' she asked.

'Yeah,' I said, wanting to laugh, and then wanting to exclaim how brilliant, and then needing, really needing, to ask one more time for the record, 'You are serious, right? You are not just making that up? If you are, I can tell you it would be a great line in a sitcom.'

'Nancy,' she said, and looked at me long over her glasses.

So, I said, 'Fantastic!' And we dropped it, and picked up Bret from school.

I thought about that little exchange a lot over the years. Bret and Jill are grown-up now, and they seem unbelievably emotionally healthy to me, but who am I to say? And I am virtually certain they have never had therapy. But, again, how would I know? (If I am right, though, I wonder whether they got the savings they did not spend on therapy and celebrated royally their against-the-odds mental health.)

But I can tell you that whatever it takes to stop trying to point all of life's notes towards the coda, and instead to take joy in the movement from one guessed-at step to another, and to produce a slew of unfinished symphonies is fantastic.

Take celebrations, for example. Completion, it seems, is the only thing worthy of celebration. We are allowed to celebrate birthdays, graduations, puberty, marriages, publication, prizes and elections. But these are all acts of completion. You either reach puberty or you don't; you graduate or you don't; you marry or you don't; the baby is either born or it isn't; you are elected or you aren't. These are recognized completions.

On the other hand, we don't celebrate the experiment we did in chemistry class that blew up but taught us about that little unstable exponent on the carbon molecule; or the radishes we planted that rotted but taught us about slope and sun; or the job we didn't get but taught us loads about an imaginative CV.

We don't celebrate our first heartbreak, which introduced us to the need for honesty with ourselves. We don't celebrate the publisher's rejection that showed us the genius of persistence. And we don't celebrate the client we lost, even though that episode shifted our vision profoundly from what others want us to want, to what we do want.

This is perverse. This is a world focusing on mistakes, mess, loose ends and unpredictability as bad. But we obey, striving, striving, striving for completion. Completion in this big sense should not be striven for or even aimed at. By nature life is mutating, morphing, moving on – all of the time. The universe is expanding and will never sit down and shut up. We and our context are movement only. Democritus was right when he observed that change is the only constant: 'We never step into the same river twice,' he said. We and the river change, and change each other.

Completion, on the other hand, by definition is static. It is over. So life, which is changing and growing and shedding and budding all at once, is inherently incomplete. Seeking completion all of the time is probably, technically, pathological.

So I propose that we examine our lives for the teeth marks of completionism. We will find these in the reversed paths toward our dreams. We conceived the dreams; we plotted a route; we even began to walk. Then we turned back.

What were we assuming that made us turn back? We must finish just so.

I hear versions of this story so often that some days it leaves me shattered. Do you think it is true, I ask, that you must finish just so? No, they say, finally, after thinking about it softly and long. No. It is not true.

And so, what is true, I ask? What is true, they say, life returning to their tone, is that there is no such thing as finishing. And, I say, if you knew in your heart that there is no such thing as finishing, how would you pursue your dream?

I would go back to where I turned around, they say, and I would take the next step – forward. I would keep my eyes and my thoughts on what I can do and want to do. I would be okay with no. I would expect and welcome frayed edges and creative mess along the way. I would know that if I focus only on finishing, I am not reaching far enough, risking originally enough, seeing courageously enough. In fact, I don't exist. And, they continue, I would celebrate now and all along the way. I would not wait until it is finished because it will never be. If it is, it dies.

> To embrace the unfinishable is to create life.

And that is right. We must seek to work with life's inherent movement. We need to live with a certain amount of venturing forth where the ground is shrouded and unstaked. Happiness stretches out on those grasses.

Dearest Kimberley, because you seem to me the epitome of suppleness and intelligent movement, you are probably already expert at this dance with dance. But maybe you could put this question in your shoe, just in case you get cold feet when you should be running barefooted into a wonderful new wind:

If you knew that to embrace the unfinishable is to create life, what would you do today?

If you do it, let me know.

If it makes you happy, I won't be surprised.

# Dear Kimberley

## Fourteen

### 'Hand Them The Moon'

As we began, we end – with love. In the end love is how we can be happy today.

And as far as I am concerned, 'handing a person the moon' is a nearly sublime act of love. Perhaps it is because it is the hardest. It requires us to be so completely, completely human we nearly squeak. It makes us use our reasoning cortex, at the very moment when other parts of the brain are so loud and so immediate they compel, they convince, they strobe, they fling, they cut. In those moments only a determined dominance of clean, exquisite reason can produce this kind of love, this kind of beauty, this kind of truth. In these moments, paradoxically, it is the overriding use of reason that can reintroduce the emotion of love.

Only a determined dominance of clean, exquisite reason can produce this kind of love.

'Handing people the moon' is the act of saying hard things so that the other person can think well while they hear them.

It is saying what is painful by striding over the pain and choosing words and tone and pace and facial expression that say, 'You matter more to me than my pain in this moment. I think you are good and intelligent, and I believe we can solve this beautifully so that we both are happy.'

I came across this phrase when I watched a friend deal with a furious colleague. When her colleague finally drew breath, my friend said, 'Ben, I think I can listen better if you can take the reproach out of your voice.'

There was a sudden silence. And my friend went on, 'See if you can say all you need to say to me as if you were handing me the moon.'

That suggestion dramatically changed not only Ben's tone, but also his words and his pacing and the look on his face. And the quality of his thinking. My friend relaxed, visibly. And at the end of her colleague's turn, she responded imaginatively, with humility and from an open heart. They found a way forward on the issue. Both eventually were happy.

I have thought a lot about that conversation. It has led me to notice how quickly a person's tone and words and pacing can cut off the other person's capacity to listen, to think, to respond intelligently. We cannot think well when we are raging or sad; and so we need to find ways to speak to people so that they do not hurt as we speak. And that is the challenge.

We need to decide to think, to slow down, to look at the person warmly and to use words that get at the issue and offer respect. Our cortex can do that. But in the moments when we are furious (from the assumption that we have no choice in this moment) or sad (from the assumption that we do not matter), deciding rationally to construct a response that flings to the side our pain and emerges wholly centre-stage with a beautiful, reasoned reply is precisely to decide to love. And thus we witness the uncompromising suppleness of being human.

But isn't this, you might well ask, a disingenuous act, a bludgeoning of authenticity? If we feel angry, scared, sad, shouldn't we 'be honest' and 'tell it like it is'? I don't think it is solely the pain that comprises who we are in that moment. Who we are is splendidly stratified. Pain is only one tier. It is the most attention-seeking, the loudest, the brashest, the most lacking in nuance and accuracy. But it is only one.

The deepest, and thus the most dependably rooted and trustworthy, response is not pain. It is love.

It is our love of the core of the other person, our love of the soon-to-appear good path between us, love of our mutual intelligence, love of an emergent happiness. This love is our most authentic self. Love macerates and unifies all of the disparate pieces of our self.

We have access to this through reason. Even in the katabatic winds between us, we have access. Our cortex is ready; it is a work of art; we can count on it. But we have heroically to call on it first.

We have to love our choice to produce a good outcome more than we love our pain. We have to love when the drug of adrenaline, the illusion of threat and the assumption of disaster are spinning us around so fast we think we are no longer spinning. As your dad taught me, when we land a C-141 transport plane in fog, we have to trust our instruments. If we trust the 'seat of our pants', we crash. In every charged and obscured interaction, mechanical or human, it is the love of our instruments, our reason, that we must trust if we want to arrive safely on the ground.

Thus we witness the uncompromising suppleness of being human.

We do land safely if it is the moon we give as we fly.

Love is not just this letter. It is every letter. Love begins us and ends us.

It is love with which I offer you these answers to your penetrating and important question.

And it is certainly in loving you that I know how to be happy today.

# Postscript

## Dear Kimberley, Hattie and Meghan

Thank you. Thank you for your questions. Thank you for your young wisdom in wondering about such big issues, and for your grown-up generosity in sharing the journey. You have made us all think. And you have shown us with your lives that thinking for ourselves, whatever our age, is both rare and irreplaceable. Life wants us to be smart navigators, courageous and kind all at once. Life loves your questions and the firing of its fine minds to consider them. Thank you for this gift.

# Appendices

# Index

# Acknowledgements

I am grateful first of all to Kimberley Crespo, Meghan Cassidy and Hattie Bremner for being brilliant young girls who are now extraordinary women, and for their generosity in wanting these letters for them to become letters for the world.

My husband, Christopher Spence, loved the letters and believed in them, and in me and my goddaughters, from the beginning. He also indefatigably engaged with the manuscript, enriching its detail and accuracy and impact.

Noemi Fabry, very early on, treated the letters as gems and convinced me that a publisher one day would treat them that way, too. Justin Davis-Smith, also very early on, gave me confidence that men, not just women, would love the letters, when he wrote to say that he missed his Tube stop, immersed as he was in reading them.

Ruth McCarthy professionally championed the project with confidence and influence, leading me to Wanda Whitely whose excitement about the letters buoyed me, and whose insistence that the letters deserved a fine agent led to Sheila Crawley of Curtis Brown Group.

Sheila's embrace of the letters and her irrepressible perseverance and game-changing lateral thinking led to Cassell and to Denise Bates, Director of Publishing for Cassell. Denise, also my editor and a deeply perceptive, imaginative, generous person, has been for me a natural, continuous Thinking Environment.

Ruth McCarthy also proposed the general title *Living With Time To Think*, a leap that made the project fly.

My sister, Merl Glasscock, was, as she always is, an unbroken line of support for me. So was my friend Vanessa Helps who has been actively at the heart of my experience as a writer since 1992.

And then there was Pierreponts Café of Goring-on-Thames. I wrote much of the final manuscript there. It is a writer's paradise.

I thank you all.

# Nancy Kline

Nancy Kline is founder and president of Time To Think, an international leadership development and coaching company. Nancy is the pioneer of the Thinking Environment®, a framework in which people can think for themselves with rigour, imagination, courage and grace. She teaches courses in this process and leads the Time To Think global faculty. She also is an acclaimed public speaker.

Nancy's other books include *Time To Think: Listening to Ignite the Human Mind* and *More Time To Think: A Way of Being in the World*.

Nancy, an American, lives in England with her British husband, Christopher Spence.

www.timetothink.com

# TIME
# TO
# THINK

## LISTENING TO IGNITE

## THE HUMAN MIND

"Do not be fooled by the simplicity of this process.
It will unleash the power of your whole organization."

*British Telecom*

## NANCY KLINE

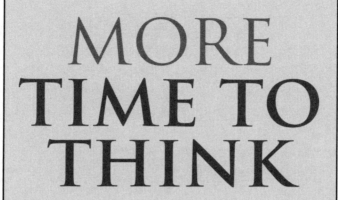

# MORE
# TIME TO
# THINK

## THE POWER OF
## INDEPENDENT THINKING

Bestselling author of *Time to Think*

NANCY KLINE